Palermo

Palermo

by
Roberto Alajmo

Translated from the Italian by
Guido Waldman

 ArmchairTraveller

First published in Great Britain in 2010 by
The Armchair Traveller at the bookHaus Ltd.
70 Cadogan Place
London SW1X 9AH
www.hauspublishing.com

This first paperback edition published in 2017

ISBN: 978 1 909961 49 4

Typeset in Garamond by MacGuru Ltd
Printed and bound in the UK

Contents

1

Welcome to the city

You have to get yourself a window seat and arrive on a clear, sunny day. These occur even in winter, because the city is always anxious to look good, whatever the season. As the aircraft begins its descent, you can see from the window the red rocks of Terrasini, and the sea aquamarine and blue, with no way of telling where the blue ends and the aquamarine begins. Even the houses, the so-called villini, may strike you as over abundant, but from up above they don't look as clumsy and pretentious as they do when seen from the ground. You take all of this in and imagine you've been put down in the most beautiful spot on the planet. Be honest, you thought you had some inkling of the city and the island because it is hard to escape clichés; but when faced with the view of the coastline by the airport you have to drop every pre-conceived idea.

As you look out of the window you have time to formulate such thoughts, to melt at the sight of so much beauty, even to entertain the notion of dropping everything – work, family, roots – and coming to settle hereabouts. And just when you're all agog with the idea of everlasting summer, along comes a countermand. This comes as usual from the window because, while you are still wholly taken up with sunlight and sea, all of a sudden a mountain surges up, a huge, grey mountain into which at any moment the aircraft seems bound to crash.

The airport at Punta Raisi is built on a narrow strip of land separating the sea from the mountain; indeed, before now, one plane has fetched up against the mountain (5 May 1972) and another in the sea (23 December 1978). That's the city airport for you. That's the city for you. You, the traveller, knew all about this before you set out, but the dazzling beauty of the landscape made you forget. Now you find yourself in a bit of a panic because the mountain is getting closer, and that is a worry. But relax, nothing will happen because today's pilots can judge to a nicety how to pass along the available strip between sea and mountain. In your subsequent moment of relief you will have leisure to reflect on the fact that nothing in these parts is what you would expect at first glance. Which is not to say you can give yourself up to the contemplation of beauty as if we were in Polynesia or Tuscany. Here, there's nothing to be relied on, and indeed it is precisely when you think you've reached nirvana that you get a whack across the chest, one to take your breath away and force you to establish a proper distance from your surroundings.

The pilot's problem on landing – how to avoid the twin disasters of sea and mountain – is a metaphor for the daily difficulties arising out of simply living on the island in general and in the city in particular; beyond being the island's capital, the city is also a sort of large-scale exasperation. Better therefore never to relax but to be forever on your guard. From one moment to the next something irretrievable might occur.

Once you've picked up your luggage – and not even this is a doddle at Punta Raisi, not as bad as landing but almost – take a taxi and keep your eyes skinned. Often you can understand a city simply by taking transport from the airport to the city centre. If you can't manage a fuller acquaintance – maybe you're only stopping over between flights – all you need is to take a taxi there and back. On the motorway you meet a good part of what the city, consciously or unconsciously, wants you to know about her. Not everything, nor all that spontaneously. But if you keep your eyes open there is at least something you can grasp. Between the airport and the city centre you'll pick up a visiting card to the city. There are towns which know what they're about – they're self-conscious and make sure to present the best picture of themselves. And there are towns that don't give a hoot about their self-image and leave everything to chance. The city falls into this second category. Even chance, however, keeps a trick up its sleeve, and within a few kilometres it will have seen to providing at least three focal points.

The first of them comes almost at the start. Looking left, seawards, more or less at Carini, you'll find a shanty town built right on the beach. The rundown condition of the huts, the fact that they seem to be made out of bits and pieces found on a tip, all rusted away, makes you think this has to be an illegal site. People obliged to live in Third World conditions. You are even enti-tled to think that somebody will have pulled a fast one, making a virtue out of necessity: as they had to make a roof over their heads, a place to sleep, why not make it by the seaside? But no, it's nothing to do with housing need: these shacks are the second homes of the city-dwellers – the places where the urbanites move to in the summer for their holidays.

In due course they came to be built in 'Cowboy Style'. Nowadays anyone trying to be witty calls it 'creative architecture', though the term is gradually losing its ironic overtone, so that before long 'creative architecture' will become an accepted designation. The walls are not plastered because there'll always be time for that later on. The metal struts stick out from the roof because, who knows, one fine day a second storey may be added for the daughter who's getting married. The houses remain unfinished on the outside for various reasons – some of them practical others, let's say, aesthetic. Meanwhile, all that is awaited is a stamp of official approval which will serve to put the place beyond the reach of criticism by the fiscal authorities. At all events, indoors is one thing and the outside quite another.

On the island, what happens a yard away from one's front door is considered irrelevant, if not downright vulgar. To check this out, just go and visit a condominium. Any condominium, even one where the rich live. After six in the evening each flat will have a wee garbage bag sitting on the ground just outside the door. In the preceding hours the bag will have been filling up, until the worthy lady of the house gets to parcelling it up and banishing it to beyond the sacred circle of the dwelling.

4

At the earliest moment the trash will be passed into the care of the community, be it only the neighbourly community represented by the outside landing of a condominium. Once the bag is closed and its neck tied, it is no longer any concern of the inhabitants. Trash is the preserve of the public authorities. The house must not be desecrated by the world's garbage. Thus you may bet that the internal arrangements of the beach houses at Cinisi are quite meticulous, in total contrast with the exterior. How things look on the outside is not the problem of these homeowners, they couldn't care less. The outside is rubbish, and as such is up to the state.

But there is another reason why these houses are so seedy-looking. The city-dwellers nurse a heathen aversion to anything that smacks of completeness. If they inaugurate a theatre, they always do so in the absence of some essential requisite to make it fully functioning. If it's a dyke they are constructing, then the conduits will remain uncompleted. Completion? We'll get round to it in due course, when and if we can.

Beneath this systematized inconclusiveness we may discover an ancestral profile of superstition. It would almost seem that the city-dwellers have an unconscious sense that total completion carries with it an inbuilt sorrow. The ancient belief that fulfilment may attract the Evil Eye of the envious survives to this day, but there's more to it than that. The real worry arises out of the discomfort of not possessing something which you thought you did possess, once you have actually realized all your hopes. There's always something that slips through even the tiniest mesh in the net we have made with our own hands. So why not wait just to see how things turn out? For all we know it could be an Arab net. In the perfection of the carpets they wove, the old Persian master-weavers always introduced a tiny error. They did this precisely in order not to challenge God in an area which was within his exclusive jurisdiction: perfection. But here, in these seaside houses at Cinisi, this form of devotion has clearly been carried to excess.

Some years ago, there was a mayor who tried to get them knocked down despite the complaints of their owners. When these owners appeared on television it was clear that they did not conform to the image of shanty-town dwellers. They didn't look like people who broke the law because they were driven to it. Rather they were solid citizens in possession of all the means, cultural and economic, to fight their corner. In fact the people from City Hall just had enough time to pull down a couple of these dwellings in front of the television cameras before the demolition stopped. At the next election the incumbent mayor did not get back in, there were changes in City Hall, and that was the last anybody heard about demolitions.

As a well prepared traveller you're bound to know that in the city and its outskirts, unauthorized building is just about the only venture in urban development of recent years. Downtown, and on the shore side in particular, the bylaws are singularly strict and nobody risks any construction work, except for those ne'er-do-wells who have no scruples. Leaving aside the new Palace of Justice, there has, since the war ended, been scarcely a single architectural development of any worth, whether public or private. The rule of thumb being that there must be no contamination between ancient and modern. The result of this rule is that here we have the first and only generation in human history that will have left no trace of its passage on earth. At least, nothing of any distinction. When, a thousand years from now, art historians look into the architectural styles obtained between the years 1900 and 2000, there'll be no getting away from the answer: jerry-building. Or else pagodas. For there are pagodas as well. Once you're in town you'll see plenty of them, to the point of assuming that they are called for in a clearly determined piece of landscaping – they are all the same, and all of them white.

The Greeks have left us the perfect model for their temples. The Romans perfected their ideal of the amphitheatre. The Byzantines their basilicas. The Arabs aqueducts and mosques. The Normans their churches with small domes. The Spaniards Gothic-Catalan portals. From the baroque era we celebrate the splendour of the oratories designed by Giacomo Serpotta. The nineteenth century left us the severe tranquillity of those urban house fronts. And in the same way, today's urban dwellers of our city will bequeath to posterity some proof of the level of architectural civilization achieved. I mean that after 10,000 years' evolution of taste along the shores of the Mediterranean, they have been able to elaborate something original and progressive: pagodas.

Were the island to fall to ruin or be swallowed up, if every memory of it were erased, and in 2,000 years' time archaeologists brought to light the ruins of the inhabited quarters, here is the name by which they would call our culture: The Pagoda Civilization. This would be a reference not to the Chinese Palace, still in existence, but rather to the gazebos in the shape of a white pagoda that populate every corner of the city. Above all, being made of plastic, the pagoda is not readily biodegradable, and future generations of archaeologists will have ample leisure to study the Pagoda Effect in all its most intriguing manifestations.

The plastic pagoda is to the inhabitants of the city what those dry-stone round towers, the nuraghe, are to the Sardinians. They are what the huge stone heads are to the Easter Islanders. What the conical-roofed house, the trullo, is for the peasant civilization of Apulia. What the igloo is to the Innuit. There is not a garden, piazza, car park, or seafront promenade that is free of them. Wherever there is space, sooner or later there will be a pagoda. It has become a conditioned reflex of urban development, a form of *horror vacui*. Every gap in the fabric of urban development, every sea view is now experienced as a sort of embarrassing rip in the seat of our trousers, and the pagoda represents the ideal patch.

Whether its object is to sell gifts or books, whether it plays host to a review of artistic objects or paintings, or is a place where charities collect signatures or contributions, a pagoda will always be the favoured framework. Indeed the only one. The pagoda is convenient. It is easy to put up and might easily be dismantled. *Might*, I say, because we have no solid information about any such thing, given that the pagoda of its nature tends to stay put. It beds itself in. It fosters squatters' rights on the public land on which it has been erected. If one is put up to serve as a toy stall for 2 November, there's little point in pulling it down with the New Year's festivities coming along, when it can be used for Christmas decorations and cribs. After that there's the carnival: masks and make-believe shit. After that, Easter: eggs and doves. On to summer: lifebelts and canoes. Before you know it, it's autumn, and the everlasting cycle of the pagoda can begin again, now and for ever and ever. You just have to take it on board and get used to it. It is for this that in future we, today's inhabitants of the city, will be remembered – for the pagoda and for unauthorized building with a sea view.

What you see as you flash past along the motorway is a string of rotting houses, somewhat reminiscent of a set of teeth that have gone badly wrong. The dentist has tried extracting a decayed tooth, and through the gap you get an occasional glimpse of the sea. On its own, the sea would be a happy sight. But the impression created by the gaps is, if possible, even worse than the worst of the building blight that is standard along the coast. With the house pulled down, only a part of the resultant rubble has been carted away, nobody has got round to a proper site clearance. That is why the gaps through which you may see the sea are painful indeed – they are the memorial of a lost battle. They are a reminder that there was a time when certain battles were worth fighting, maybe even worth winning.

Many a battle of this kind has been fought in the city. Just as many are the involuntary monuments which stand as a record of them. Another memorial of a lost battle is to be found a few kilometres further, on the right, at Capaci.

Up until a few years ago, when people were chatting in the car, or anyone was chatting on the road between Punta Raisi and the city, there was always a sudden pause. That was when one was passing by the red-painted guard-rail. If there was a visitor on hand, he would be warned of it a couple of dozen yards short of it: 'Look, we're about to pass the spot where the assassination attempt took place.' Then, the silence. It was a moment's silence during which everyone would recollect where he was that day, what he was doing. Then the pause would end and the conversation resume.

But that stretch of road has changed. They've put up an obelisk on either side with names, date, the lot. Often there's still the wreath left there from the previous 23 May, and, as the flowers wilt in a few days, even this detail serves to depress the majesty of the scene.

In time, the two obelisks and the withered wreath have become part of the scene. Passing in front of them, people no longer feel the need to stop talking. One gets used to things. At the most there is a brief moment's reflection on what we were doing, how much time has passed, and so forth. That's normal. It is the normal elaboration of grieving, especially when the state has assumed the task of recollection by means of monuments and ceremonies.

And yet there is a sense of guilt that is very much of the island. After each Mafia crime, usually on the anniversary, it has us asking ourselves rather foolishly: 'Was his death really needless?' As if there were some utilitarian purpose for a person's death. As if it were possible to establish some threshold of utility beyond which there was no point dying. As if death could be weighed on the scales. As if death were a commodity for sale. As if there were an exchange and mart for death. As if there were some other commodity that might be offered in exchange for a person's death.

Up to a point yes; however, it seemed possible to say, *a posteriori*, that there was a difference between the deaths of Falcone and Borsellino. However disgusting it may seem, there was a fair amount of time during which many people felt that those deaths could, at a pinch, be considered *not needless*. Between 1992 and 1994 this utilitarian approach found an application, for once, that was positive, with the revolt against the Mafia. For two years the city persuaded itself that it was prefiguring a better future for the whole of Italy. They always say that it is in the city that things happen first. True, they happen all too blatantly. Then one section of the city-dwellers asked themselves: why can't a moral revolution start right here?

Prior to 1992, the general practice was to delegate the war against the Mafia. Judges and policemen were sent to their deaths, and then there would be a lather of indignation over their demise. Thereafter, the parabola of indignation began its descent, in parallel with the indignation of the state, until everything evaporated and nothing was left. The anniversary was kept, a trial was instituted which served to prolong the memory simply by the length of time it took, and in the end everything reverted to the normal business of survival, of live and let live.

To understand why the murders of Falcone and Borsellino marked a turning point that led to the first, authentic, unique and brief anti-Mafia revolt, we perhaps have to go back to August 1991, when Libero Grassi was murdered. Compared with the others, Grassi was a unilateral anti-Mafia member of parliament. He was entirely on his own. He had received no official commission. He was neither a policeman nor a magistrate. He was not professionally engaged in the fight against the Mafia, and he wasn't paid for it. He was not even the first member of parliament in the history of the war against the Mafia; but he was the first one to use the mass media. He made his denunciations on television, safe in the conviction that this was for him tantamount to a life insurance policy. Here he miscalculated, as witness the fact that he was killed, indeed that he *had* to be killed, precisely due to the publicity he had given his denunciations. Libero Grassi wanted to be an example so as to encourage honest businessmen, and he was killed in order to destroy such an example.

On the morning when they shot him he was on his own, and he was virtually alone at his funeral, when the city skulked behind her shutters, as shown in so many Mafia movies. This time, however, it was not a conspiracy of silence, it was shame. The city was ashamed of herself because the motive for the crime had been made all too clear thanks to the use Libero Grassi had made of the mass media. On that occasion nobody could simply look the other way. Not even the Mafia and its associates could resort to the trick of playing the thing down to the point of non-existence – weaving a web of fatalism and posthumous defamation, the trick normally employed. Only on this occasion it did not work, because the motive had some time back been broadcast to the public. This was the first time that the city could not help being ashamed of herself, like a cat who's had its faced rubbed into the carpet where it's relieved itself in the corner of the sitting room.

Note well, however, this was the shame of a person who will never admit that he has anything to be ashamed of. There and then nothing emerged from among Libero Grassi's fellow businessmen, who continued blithely to pay the indemnity to the Mafia. Rather it was a slow revolution, from the bottom up; it was a moral revulsion in which the ruling classes, the business community, the politicians, had only a marginal role.

The two assassinations of 1992 were the first occasion for the city's sense of shame to find expression, though it had already started to ferment in her stomach. The sense of shame took the form of a demonstration, the fermentations in civil society came to the surface in the lower-middle-class strata, those with few responsibilities. They came out into the street in their masses, and their message was pretty much the same: Enough is enough!

And as it was in those days, half the world's press corps were there in the city, all waiting to see whether there might be further slaughter, the anti-Mafia processions and the committee that hung sheets from windows becoming the opening item for the television news, for lack of anything better. After the demonstration everyone went home and watched themselves on television, recognized themselves in the procession, noted that at least on television they made quite a crowd, and were back in the streets the next day and the day after, reflecting themselves to infinity in the media mirror of their own indignation. For the first time the city saw a positive picture of herself in the papers she read. How nice! For a couple of years it seemed possible that something might come out of it, that something was about to happen any day now. At a certain point it even looked as if something really was happening.

There was a long interval during which policemen of whatever description stopped behaving like crooks. Before this, when a couple of lads on a moped spotted a police patrol beyond the bend, one of the two would say: 'The fuzz!' Or worse in their dialect, a locution that lies somewhere between 'Look out!' and 'Bugger off!' However, in the couple of years after the slaughter, when the lads without motorcycle helmets spotted a patrol car beyond the bend, they might have had the same reaction, but what they would say was merely 'Police!' They would feel in the wrong and try slipping off down a side-turning, but what they meant when they shouted 'Police!' was merely police. In any event, the children of the well-to-do middle classes no longer alluded to the forces of order as 'The Fuzz': they would say 'The Police'.

This may seem trifling, but it is not. If there was a change, this lexical evolution provided the best indication of it: the young lads no longer observed the police as a hostile element. The police were now a force that one might approach with a measure of guarded confidence. The officials of the state had become co-belligerents. This resulted from the radicalization of the clash between the Mafia and the Rest of the World, following the predominance of Cosa Nostra's assassination wing.

Previous generations had talked of 'the Fuzz' not because these were made up of hardened delinquents, but because of where they came from. They came from the Savoy kingdom, they came from the Bourbons; and further back still, going back through the remoter genealogy of domination, the Fuzz were the representatives of Phoenician power. Then, at a certain point, for the first time, 140 years after the landing of Garibaldi's Thousand, this was no longer the case. For a moment it looked as if something had changed that had never changed in 3,000 years.

Of course this change only affected the middle class, and of course it did not apply to every representative of that class. It did not apply to those who had far worse sins to conceal than that of riding on a moped, two up, with no helmet. The degree of connivance between organized crime and the business community remained all too high. The achievements arrived at in the field of culture were undeniable, but they remained ends in themselves, divorced from any effort to incorporate them into the commercial sector. A businessman who wanted to invest in the island still had to confront the dilemma of choosing between connivance and heroism. And this is not the kind of courage that is to be prescribed to an investor.

Any great leap forward had to be ascribed to the will to overcome this obstacle, if not ascribable to demagogy pure and simple. But the moral revulsion that arose out of the assassinations was a little flame that had to be kept sheltered from the rain. Because after the summer it started to rain again as usual. The police went back to being called 'the Fuzz' and all reverted to what it had been before.

To put it simply, the moral revulsion began immediately after the assassinations and its end began with Leoluca Orlando's election as mayor. That was the time needed to elaborate the grieving and it ended with a new delegation of power on the old model. Just one difference: the delegation was now not to the magistracy alone but to the entire political class. Society decided for once to elect a politician a little better than itself, entrusting to him the task of combating the Mafia. But not only that: the new generation of bureaucrats was required to supply answers to each and every point at issue, vital and peripheral. So much was obvious and possible, but also veered towards the impossible. There were enormous expectations made of Orlando. He became the patron saint of the city. Whatever happened, for good or ill, was laid at Orlando's door. And of course Orlando was eventually blamed for not having been able to keep the flame of hope alive. No account was made for the fact that, except in brief intervals, hope is not what is required of a mayor and his wife: what is sought is reliability and constancy. For a long time the myth was nurtured of a city reborn, but this renaissance impelled from on high became the alibi for a general disengagement. After the so-called spring in the city there followed a miserable summer – miserable, but still summer – with the sheets hung from the window and the human chains. Then came a sunny autumn, and after that a winter in which society pulled in its horns.

To know how it all ended up, just give the journey time to complete its course. Here is the taxi coming off the motorway, engaging upon the ring-road. And here the third indication is to be found, the third trace that the city has left of herself along the initial path traced by each visitor. It is a phantom trace, because it is no longer there. Had you arrived a few years ago, maybe you would have spotted it. I mean with your own eyes. It was a yellow sign that had been by the roadside for years. Now all you can do is try to imagine it. On the yellow sign were the words in black letters:

**ELECTRIC LIGHTING SWITCHED OFF TO
CONFORM TO SAFETY REGULATIONS.**

Especially if you come to a traffic jam you'll have plenty of time to imagine and reflect upon it. The words did not say 'for <u>work in progress</u> to conform ...', but precisely 'switched off to conform to safety regulations'. In other words, according to the notice, safety regulations required the electric lighting to be switched off. Not that there was any sign of work to this effect. Nor had there ever been any such work available to view or within the memory of man.

There were in fact days when the sign was up at a point in the road where the lights were working perfectly normally, and anyone passing by would ask, 'Why switched off? Which lights? Conformity to what?' You too, being a thoughtful traveller, will be putting these questions to yourself. And in search of impossible answers, you'll realize that this notice offered more than meets the eye. It reached beyond mere questions of street lighting. Although it was a moveable sign, it stayed in the one place so long that, now it is no longer there, its ghost may be considered a part of the landscape. Its moral shade has remained to keep its memory green. And quite right too, for that yellow sign was a perfect example of one typical aspect of the city: an aspect that might be defined as a *tendency to settle for the worst.*

Here's an example: if a new recruit turns up in an office with the intention of getting some work done, that person will very soon be isolated and neutralized. A cordon sanitaire of workmates will form around him, people who do no work and won't have anyone doing any work in their place. A crazy maverick in the office could upset the output of the place: this has to be put to a stop at all costs. Before many months have elapsed the Stakhanovite will have been restored to common sense and placed in a position where he can play a full part in reducing the office output.

Here's another example: when an air raid destroyed one of the two splendid pillars of Porta Felice, the city-dwellers did not immediately see to rebuilding it, but out of an instinct of abject symmetry their thought was to knock down the other one, the one left standing. In the end they did nothing, but in such cases just the thought is enough to give one the idea.

Similarly, if a theatre has a problem with its electrics, there will be much discussion as to the best electrician to call in, and which method to use. In the meantime the theatre will be closed, out of safety considerations. This is precisely what happened with the Teatro Massimo, the city's opera house, which remained dark for almost a quarter of a century before they found an electrician up to the task of sorting out the problem. Which does not even go into the whole tangle of problems that meanwhile arose out of the theatre being closed for safety reasons.

Once again: if a party or candidate decides to seize the votes of the illegals or of the tax-evaders, at once all the others will hasten to follow them down the same path. They will make up to illegals and tax-evaders for their own electoral advantage. From which one may argue that all parties and candidates are the same, so one might just as well vote for the one that gets into the racket first or that does it on the grander scale.

There is no shortage of examples but here, in brief, is what the *tendency to settle for the worst* consists of: if in doubt, always go for the worst solution. In the city this tendency has reached levels of application that in other places would not even be dreamed of. Here Murphy's Law is guaranteed by the Constitution. Summits and conferences will be arranged to establish what will be the worst resolution for the principal requirements. If something can go wrong, a committee will be formed, a task force will be set up, an armed escort will be provided; anything to guarantee that whatever it is turns out as badly as can be.

In Via Rocca Pirri there is a church, Santa Maria dei Naufragati, St Mary of the Shipwrecked. Not that anyone in that area calls it that. Everyone calls it Annegati, St Mary of the Drowned. In other words: it never occurs to anyone that shipwreck could lead to anything like rescue. Not a hope that the shipwrecked person might survive by reaching shore safe and sound. Shipwreck = Drowning. So one may just as well entrust the Madonna with the salvation of the shipwrecked person's soul.

You, newly arrived visitor, these are things you have to know; so when you are told about the typical pessimism that obtains on the island, you will understand that it is a self-generated pessimism. A smug pessimism that feeds upon itself to the point of becoming a systematic pursuit of the worst. If you think that something must go wrong, there is every likelihood that it *will* go wrong. The more you concentrate, the more you force yourself to imagine how things could get even worse, the more things will unfailingly get worse. And it is right that you should know this from the moment you arrive in the city. Considering the yellow notice at the entrance to the ring-road will serve the purpose of putting you on your guard. In practice, it is the equivalent to a sign that, oddly enough, is nowhere to be found along the road: welcome to the city.

2

Commonplaces

Here comes the difficulty, however. Everything mentioned in the previous chapter, added to everything you have heard over the years, the months, the weeks and days of your life have left you feeling a shade apprehensive. As the day of departure draws near, there is always somebody ready to put you on your guard. The city could not be more beautiful, alive, fascinating, BUT ... In the preparatory homework there was always a BUT, an antithetical formula that has turned your anticipation of the journey into a worried ambivalence. On the one hand the urge to go no matter what, on the other the fear of getting the worst of it – possibly, if not probably. All kinds of fantastic stories are told about the city. Fantastic in both senses: marvellous and at the same time deriving from fantasy. So much so that your poor traveller's head, barely arrived in a place that is strange to you, is so full of conflicting information you no longer know what to think.

I can understand you. This is why, once you have reached your hotel, after unpacking, after you've put your things carefully away in the cupboard, you shilly-shally over something to keep you busy so that everything in the room is perfectly sorted. Let's be honest: you're a trifle nervous.

Here you are shut up in your hotel room and in no hurry to leave it. All that talk about the Mafia. About small-time crooks. About the traffic. About the savagery of which the city is capable when she puts her mind to it. All so many poisons that have entered your bloodstream drop by drop, and are now in the process of infecting you. Here you are in a place you've never been to before, a totally unknown place so far as you are concerned, and yet you feel you know it all too well. And not everything you know about it is all that agreeable. Some things yes, else you'd not have come. But others don't appeal to you in the least.

You look out of the window and see a small stretch of street. There is a traffic jam, which corresponds to your own idea of the city. But a minute portion of so complex a whole is not sufficient to confirm all the ideas you have accepted and crammed into your head. All manner of ideas, which combine to reflect back on you a bewildering notion of the city and its inhabitants. Now, come clean: the predominant notion is of a positively dangerous city. But that is not the only reason why you hesitate to leave your room. The fact is that your accepted ideas are so many and so layered that you are in no hurry to go and test them out for yourself. To be more specific, you have two fears that are symmetrical and contradictory: that your ideas prove to be wrong, and that your ideas prove to be right. The more you think about it, the less you can decide which of the two is the worse. Let me try to set your mind at rest: it is not unusual for the city to provoke this effect of simultaneous attraction and repulsion. This is normal enough. I should like to explain how it can happen that such simple commonplaces can be so upsetting, but the explanations that come to mind are themselves, alas, commonplaces in their turn.

One normally knows from the outset, for example, that the inhabitants fall into categories – they love the whole idea of categories. One notable double category is: leavers and stayers. There's been much debate surrounding this. There's a whole literature concerning the 'islanders on the rock' and the 'islanders on the open sea'. The leavers consider the stayers to be rustics destined for the worst kind of existential bankruptcy, while the stayers speak of the leavers as deserters who have abandoned the front line to take refuge at the rear.

Each of these factions, of course, harbours its own secret misgivings. The stayers wake up every morning wondering whether they have done the right thing to stay. They open the window, look out at the sunshine, have breakfast, with one eye on the ricotta, and conclude that OK, they've done the right thing. At the same moment, the leavers wake up, open the window, see a grey sky, breakfast on a desiccated pastry out of the freezer and fear they have made a big mistake. The same is true in their corresponding daily routines, and little by little their thoughts come to coalesce. At the end of the day, the stayer will have to admit that he got it all wrong, and the leaver will take comfort in his standard of living which is, when all's said and done, something gained, at least from the point of view of employment.

This is why among the stayers it is possible to identify two subdivisions: those who toy with the idea of leaving and those who toy with the idea of not leaving. The stayer often devotes his life to planning to leave. He keeps up contacts, makes sure to stay in touch with the rest of the world. He never stops digging out the tunnel which some day or other might allow him to leave the city. Vice versa, there are those who are perfectly content where they are, entirely content with what the city has to offer. They even reach the point of finding positive things to say about the city's drawbacks. No work? So much the better: all the more time to enjoy the Mondello sunshine in peace.

In the same way, the leavers may be subdivided into two categories: those dreaming of a return, and those who have no such thought. You yourself, traveller, will know many people from the city who have been living elsewhere for years but who still, despite the passage of time, are forever on the look out for a pastry shop where they make cream horns the way they remember them from their childhood. There are those who, on discovering that you're going to be in their city, get you to promise to bring back for them at any rate a bunch of wild fennel, the shamanic ingredient that will allow them another try at preparing pasta with pilchards while away from the island; the experiment is not unlike trying to breed pandas in captivity. At the end of all his labours the homesick cook will conclude that the pasta with pilchards as his mother made it was altogether nicer; a delicious pasta like that is not something he'll ever sample again as long as he lives.

The converse of that nostalgia is the wilfulness of the one who has left the island and proceeds ostentatiously to destroy every bridge connecting him to the past. These are the converts, the unfrocked priests. And like every unfrocked priest, the one who has left without regrets feels the need to show the world that he has buried every kind of doubt. Not content to have persuaded himself, he goes out of his way to make converts, and is quite zealous in his attempts to persuade everyone else of the horror of a life entirely spent basking in the defects of the city.

There is a false perspective concerning those inhabitants of the island who have gone abroad to seek their fortunes. The idea always is: my, aren't they on the ball, these islanders – whatever they turn their hands to they always make a go of it! In the movies, the arts, fashion, literature. What's wrong with this perspective lies in the belief that these emigrant geniuses form a representative sample of the island's inhabitants. Which is far from the case – you only have to consider the recurring historical dynamic that expects to see the cream of the island's youth periodically emigrating. From the defeat of Ducezio to the expulsion of the Jews, to the collapse of the rural uprisings, to the recent brusque reawakening of the dream of industrialization – at each critical moment the system sees a fresh distribution of society and labour which applies solely to those who are willing to knuckle under. As for the rest, for those who rebel, there are simply no jobs to be had. For the hotheads the only answer is to emigrate. That is why the diasporan islanders all seem so bright. It's because there's been a sorting out at an earlier stage. History shows that it is always the best and brightest who are forced out. So it's no surprise that the city never manages to free herself from under-development.

You are not an unintelligent traveller so you suspect that neither of the main categories – together with all the subdivisions deriving from them – in fact exhausts the dynamics of their relationship, reducing them merely to mutual resentment, indeed to mutual loathing. All categories and sub-categories have one thing in common: reciprocal envy. One and all are convinced that this city is more complicated than any other. But even this is not the end of the matter. Certainly, here the business of living is not the same as the business of living in any other city in the world, because the city-dwellers' sense of belonging is quite exceptional.

Gianni Riotta once found himself explaining that when a resident of the city happens to be travelling in any part of the world whatsoever, and is asked where he comes from, he knows straightaway that with his answer his interlocutor will unfailingly associate the name of the city with the word 'Mafia' or something along those lines. The best he can hope for is an interlocutor with a measure of discretion, who will simply say nothing. But you can bet he'll be thinking: City = Mafia.

A city-dweller is hurt by this sort of thing. Especially to begin with. Then the time comes when he gets used to it and this horrid business of City = Mafia somehow changes colour – it's not easy to explain – and becomes something of a bashful complacency. It would seem that this bashful complacency is the one form of belonging to which the city-dwellers may aspire. We are talking, though, about a very strong sense of belonging. Eventually, by dint of hearing it constantly repeated, one comes

to believe that one possesses an identity. One is somebody. A mafioso. Or an anti-mafioso.

If, beyond the numerous and convenient nuances of
connivance, there is no escaping the Mafia/anti-Mafia
dichotomy, that is because the city is a thoroughly moral
epicentre. Here you cannot engage in any business until
you have confronted a number of ethical problems. Everybody knows, if they wish to know, what they are in
for if they choose this job rather than that one, merely
from the fact that they will be working in the city. It is
different to be a magistrate or policeman, obviously, but
also a lawyer, priest, witness in a law court, tradesman,
entrepreneur, teacher, intellectual or illegal parker. Had
Libero Grassi been born in Cuneo, no one would have
heard of him, and he would have lived a while longer.
But he was not simply an entrepreneur: he was also a
city-dweller, which made matters all the worse. Just as,
conversely, to be an entrepreneur makes matters worse
for a city-dweller.

There's only one calling that may be pursued in the city
with full satisfaction, and in a certain sense even sticks
up two fingers to moral scruples: the writer or journalist. Writers and journalists are parasites who survive by
feeding off misfortune, their own and others'. Which is
why for this class of people the entire island serves as an
inexhaustible source of stories and inspiration. Nowhere
in the world is there soil that offers, in such a concentration, so broad a sampling of earthquakes, volcanic erup-
tions, Mafia, unemployment, illegal immigrants, drought,
floods (strange though it may seem, on the island the one

does not preclude the other). From the classic stockpile of literary woes all that is missing is plague. But who knows? Before too long somebody will manage to organize something of this nature.

This is why that which ties people to the island is all the stronger in writers. If you are born on the island you'll find it hard to write of anything else. You can tug on the umbilical cord as hard as you like, hoping it will break. But it never does. Often even the writers of the diaspora achieve a measure of their national and international status as they continue to speak of their native land. And this is something that happens almost exclusively among the island's writers. What elsewhere is provincialism is here transformed into a universal metaphor. Nobody would think of calling Calvino a 'Ligurian writer'. Sciascia, on the other hand, was always, even at the height of his fame, a writer 'from the island'.

The strength of a writer like Sciascia lay in his ability to firm up his roots. He continued to move around freely in the universe of human knowledge, but limited himself to using the reality of the island as a mirror to reflect the world. With all that this implies in terms of humility and patience. He had hit upon a good private solution to the dilemma of leaving or staying: he would spend four months in Paris to breathe, four months in the city to think, and four at Racalmuto, away from all distractions, to write. To have pulled up his roots, to detach his shadow from the earth, taking off to settle for good in Paris, Rome or Milan, would have involved him in losing a good part of the power of his imagination.

With writers and journalists out of harm's way, everyone else may find sufficient motive to live in the city on a purely emotional plane. Her inevitable morality makes her so attractive that often, in the eyes of one born there, any other place tends to seem tedious after a very short while. It's a bit like having learnt to run in rarefied air, or while being shot at from behind. Even in the absence of an elegant technique you run the faster, because hyperventilation, terror, adrenaline, the fight for survival, all these serve as a powerful boost to the engine. Contrariwise, in a place where the fight for survival is less of a struggle, there is the risk of running out of motivation and, after a while, abandoning the race. This is the blessed risk of those city-dwellers who live outside the diaspora. *Blessed* because even those who stay behind would, if they were honest, surrender a good dose of the picturesque in exchange for a better standard of living. Ruins are highly photogenic, but living among them is not at all the same thing as coming to pay them a visit from time to time.

Now you, a puzzled traveller standing at the window of a hotel, a hotel of middling comfort, can have no inkling of these matters. The few moments of contact you have had with the natives have been of an administrative nature. If the first impact has not left you traumatized, and if what I have been saying has not served to discourage you, you could still nurture the initial impression the city left with you as you looked from the aircraft window: that of a spot where the advantages as a place to live are quite dazzling they are so obvious. And yet in your heart you still preserve those words that put you on your guard:

29

in the short term the city can indeed be most seductive. For a week, a fortnight, a month or maybe two she is capable of displaying a well-nigh irresistible fascination. How long do you think your journey is going to take?

Perhaps a good part of her charm derives from the fact that the city is one of those that is constantly on the move. There are cities that move and cities that stand still. There are cities where one arrives knowing everything about them. You go as a tourist to obtain confirmation of what you've already heard or read about. You go, check it all out, return home and confirm to your friends and acquaintances: Yes, Venice is quite unique. Yes, Rome is the Eternal City. Yes, Paris is always Paris. More or less wittingly you go to these places in order to confirm your own identity as a world citizen, and back home you have assembled a whole baggage of clichés sufficient to keep you going until your next trip.

Back home with your friends, you can well get away with simply sighing: Ah, Paris! Ah, Rome! Ah, Venice! The sigh on its own could be sufficient to give the impression of unconditional love, and meanwhile the cliché will do very well. For the city no slogan has yet been devised as an all-purpose formula, one that can be trotted out as the perfect local cliché. Something like 'Paris is always Paris'. Though this can't be rendered as 'The City is always the City', if only because it isn't true: the city never remains equal to herself. The city is forever changing. By fits and starts, and not always for the better. But changing she always is. You go today, you were there five years ago, you'll be back in a couple of years, and she will be different each time. There are towns that can't stand still for even a minute. They keep altering their urban structure and even their own character while managing to keep their identity unaltered. This is not the case for every town. Some towns, if they are to preserve the full weight of their identity, need to remain absolutely still. Barcelona moves. Venice stands still. Havana moves. Vienna stands still. Berlin moves. The city does too. The city moves a lot. She moves so much that you'll do well to worry about the photos you'll take when you eventually leave your hotel: there's the risk that they'll all come out blurred.

The idea you've made of her, one of the ideas planted in you, is that to settle in the city you have to be a true sadomasochist. But let this not scandalize you. Aren't there people who get themselves tied up and flogged by their partner? So why should it be a problem if a person insists on living in the city? There are people who like the place, people who can't manage without it.

In any case, the everlasting dilemma for the leavers and the stayers is still unresolved; a dilemma that comes down to us from Schopenhauer and through Leopardi fetches up with Woody Allen: the choice between Horrible and Ghastly. Horrible is when you're lame or blind. Ghastly is every other condition. Be content to be only in the Ghastly class.

There now. The next thing is to establish between the leavers and the stayers which class is truly Horrible and which one must consider itself fortunate enough to be merely Ghastly.

3

Nostalgia for the city

Often, being able to get one's bearings helps do away with the resistance of an unknown place. On your first arrival in a city, it is a comfort to be able to locate the main street. The one where you can mingle with the locals and fancy that you don't look like an outsider. But even here the city is less straightforward than one might wish – in the sense that there is more than one main street. There are loads of them, some of them running off each other, others away from the centre, others specializing in a certain kind of *promenade*, for certain people and at certain hours of the day.

Let's take a look. There's Corso Vittorio Emanuele, historically the Càssaro. But the pavements are so narrow and overrun with parked cars that it's not been a promenade street for years. In olden days it was Piazza Bologni that served as the open-air drawing room, but here too the invasive parking facilities have driven out the pedestrians. What in Barcelona is the splendid *rambla*, here is Via Libertà, the street which at the end of the nineteenth century set the tone for urban residential development. And yet the central reservation, which in a proper *rambla* would be kept for pedestrians, is not readily accessible to them. Furthermore, Via Libertà gives particular evidence of the genetic mutation that has in only a few years ripped apart the fabric of the city's commerce.

Along the first stretch there is but a single café. The rest have been swept away, to be replaced with luxury boutiques, the kind that intimidate the clientele, starting with the sparseness of the goods on sale. Each shop one item. A single little suit. A little blouse. A pair of shoes. A necktie. And the prices are in inverse proportion to the sparseness. The fewer the goods, the higher the prices. Little by little this type of shop has ousted the traditional cafés where you could stop for a coffee and enjoy the spectacle of the world going by. So we have to regard Via Libertà as definitively out of the running as an authentic promenade street.

That leaves Piazza Politeama, Via Ruggero Settimo and Via Belmonte, which we shall discuss later on. But the city's chief historical avenue is Via Maqueda. Even here the compressed pavements militate against a pleasure stroll, but the street deserves a place in this narrative for a number of reasons. Via Maqueda is so called after Don Bernardino de Cardines, Duke of Maqueda, the island's Viceroy at the end of the sixteenth century. The learned pronounce it 'Makeda', but it is possible to settle for a compromise pronunciation that is less Spanish-sounding. Via Maqueda starts at the Teatro Massimo and stops at the Central Station, providing one of the two main thoroughfares in the city. The other one is Corso Vittorio Emanuele. The two form a cross that divides the historic centre into four quarters. From the crossroads emanate the four districts into which the old city is divided.

Along Via Maqueda on the right are clothes shops while on the left what you have are ... clothes shops. As we have seen with regard to Via Libertà, this is perhaps the one city in the world with the largest provision of clothes shops. It is hard to understand why this is, for these shops are not particularly inexpensive nor do they stand out for originality. They all sell exactly the same garments. The boutiques on Via Maqueda especially, which charge a little less, may virtually all be grouped together under the local label of *fetching*. The adjective *fetching* has many meanings: a general application, one for the young person, one for the rich and another for the poor. Short of knowing how to classify an object or an idea, you need only term it *fetching* and everybody understands. So this is what the Via Maqueda shops are: *fetching*, or *stylish*. Stylish and more or less empty, because no one ever goes in to buy something. It is one of the city's mysteries just how these shopkeepers get by. They never stop complaining, and occasionally they'll close their stylish boutique, only to open another stylish one with a stylish name, stick it out for six months, start complaining again, shut up shop and start again from scratch. This is the truth and maybe also the solution of the mystery: the shops in the city are continually recycling themselves.

The traffic in Via Maqueda barely stops from morning to night. Hence the stink in the air. It is such a persistent stench that anyone living in the neighbourhood grows accustomed to it and doesn't notice it. If every now and then someone discovers, with facts and figures to prove it, that the city is polluted, the inhabitants reply, 'What do you mean?' This is because they are convinced they are living in the world's most stylish city, and therefore her air cannot but be stylish as well.

All this stylishness in the air is an olfactory mass hallucination, and the proof is that the stench in Via Maqueda condenses and turns into deposits on the façades of the buildings, which look as if they've been built out of volcanic tufa. When the time comes to restore a façade they discover that it is in fact made of Aspra stone, and it comes out in an ochre colour far removed from the surrounding sootiness, to the point that it seems quite out of place. But that doesn't last long: in a few months the air takes care of it and the restored façade reverts to its sootiness and blends in with its surroundings. Another example of the *tendency to settle for the worst*.

Every now and then someone – at City Hall or on some committee or other – suggests closing Via Maqueda to traffic and making it a pedestrian zone. This is the sort of proposal that sends the Via Maqueda shopkeepers into hysterics – not least the small shopkeepers, as also the fly-by-night businesses – who don't wait for the traffic restriction to come into force before producing statistics to prove that turnover has dropped by 30 per cent. Turnover that, on their own admission, was already non-existent. And while the task proceeds of working out what zero less 30 per cent comes to, the papers carry debates on the subject of the pedestrian zone for the next two months on average, normally to coincide with the onset of the Christmas season. The shopkeepers threaten to sack their staff. The staff picket the shops to protest against the threat of redundancy. It seems that from one moment to the next a popular revolt is about to break out. Then it is Christmas, and nothing more happens, because everyone agrees that Via Maqueda is, all things considered, more stylish as it is.

One of the few pedestrian zones that have actually been brought into being is in Via Belmonte. On that occasion the papers had all produced the usual copy, with the shopkeepers already seeing themselves thrown onto the street, while the residents were all in favour as they imagined this would give them a place in the city's drawing room. The shopkeepers had argued, quite rightly, that the city-dwellers preferred to stop their cars right outside the shop, never mind whether they were double- or triple-parked, just so long as they could keep an eye on their vehicles. Even in that case there had been lock-outs and threats of redundancy. But the point is that there were no local elections coming up and City Hall was determined to stand fast; the pedestrian zone was established and it's still there. On balance, it could be said that all of them were wrong: the shopkeepers because they saw their turnover go spiralling up a thousandfold, and now they are rolling in money. And the residents as well, because the promenade along Via Belmonte, especially on Saturday and Sunday afternoons becomes a veritable pedestrian traffic jam. A place to be avoided by misanthropes and loners until the small hours.

The phenomenology of the city's traffic warrants a separate treatment. As a properly clued-up traveller you will already have heard about it, and it would be neither honest nor useful to keep the truth from you. But a word of warning: should you eventually decide to step out of your hotel, pray don't do so during the rush hour, when the traffic achieves the acme of exasperation. Above all don't ever do so on Saturday or Sunday. If the weekday traffic jam is passable, the weekend one is an irritant for philosophical reasons. You imagine that between Monday and Friday all these motorists are on the road for reasons of work, and thus because they are obliged to be there. But at weekends where do they get off to? And wherever they go, why go by car? And worst of all: why do they with their vehicles prevent me from getting any-where fast in mine?

The weekend and Friday evening bottleneck in Via Ruggiero Settimo constitutes the evolution of the public get-together which even today takes place in the villages: the stroll along the main drag. The only thing is, the city is not a village. Take care not to think so, the city-dwellers would be vexed. At a pinch it is a compromise between a country town and a metropolis. It stands mid-stream. Too provincial to give up the public get-together and too metropolitan to do it in the traditional way, on foot. So the practice takes place, but by car. Everyone shut up inside their vehicle, at a snail's pace.

If it's the traffic you're afraid of, I can understand your reluctance. A good solution of course would be to choose a hotel out of town. There are plenty of them, especially in recent years, which have opted to keep away from the centre, in the illusion that you can live in town while keeping to the open country, observing the city without getting too closely involved. Except that even an out of town hotel offers no guarantees. Sooner or later you'll have to settle accounts with the city. Everyone has to, albeit with differing expectations. Seen from a distance, the historic centre looks as though prey to a miniature continental drift, as though sliding along a fault line of its own, distinct from the suburbs, and this drift serves to distance it.

The suburbanites read the news of what goes on downtown with a measure of dread, especially the endless news regarding the traffic. They follow the developments on the urban network much as during a war one looks at the map to check how close, how absurdly close, the bombs have fallen.

In fact one gets used to it: one gets used to everything, even to the noise. One thing you have to know if you're not going to be dumbfounded when you step outside is that for motorists in the city the horn is a means of mass communication, a gadget on a par with the mobile phone, which you use to apprise people of even your most secret thoughts. Downtown one gets used to it, but if you're not used to it, each hoot of the horn is – just consult the Highway Code – the warning of an imminent danger. To discover that it is no more than exclamation mark, a show of irritation, surprise or elation by a communicative motorist does nothing to reduce your stress levels.

As a result of this derailment of the senses – smell and hearing in particular – in the city the expression 'going downtown' carries an undertone of menace not found anywhere else. 'Going downtown' as a Dantesque metaphor of descent into hell, as an initiation ordeal to be confronted with a stout heart. The voyage into the city centre comprises the dizzy fascination of the unknown. We undertake it entrusting ourselves to our spirit of adventure, for this is a voyage replete with the unexpected. We each have time to ask ourselves: should I or shouldn't I take the moped? Which streets will my bus take today? Will the tradespeople have blocked the road in order to press for a resolution of the traffic snarl-up? And those workers who fulfil some useful social function, where will they strike this time with their demonstration? Keeping ourselves informed, reading the papers, planning our journey is not enough. We have to go and check it all out in person. There was a time when using Via Maqueda at all was a matter of luck. The street could be closed, open, or optional. All depended on the traffic policeman in charge of the access that day – was he going to be strict or relaxed? The motorist had to get right up close and decide in a matter of seconds, scrutinizing the expression and comportment of the traffic officer. If he had turned to chat with a colleague, for instance, that meant you could get through. If, on the other hand, he was closely watching the traffic, it was altogether better to take note of the statutory deviation. As a rule there is no lack of barred entries but not all are unavoidable. What is refused as a right may perfectly well be conceded as an act of kindness. This in the long run breeds a sort of latent sense of guilt. And this Kafkaesque sense of guilt obtains a purchase on the city-dweller that will leave him in a permanent state of submission.

The motorist who goes downtown relying on nothing but his own strength well recognizes the dismay of discovering each time a new set of requirements and prohibitions. If he enjoys travel, this can in a way offer positive aspects, because he will always harbour the sense of travelling in a different city. He will come to new viewpoints, the one-way systems will force him to visit quarters he's never seen before, he'll get to know other motorists, and will have leisure – from the car window while the traffic is held up – to engage in the sort of conversation which the rhythms of modern life seem to have swept away but which, surprisingly, the traffic has served to recover.

It can happen in the city that you arrive at a traffic light and cannot turn either right or left (No Turning) nor go straight ahead (No Polluting Vehicles); there is nothing for it then but to make peace with your conscience and abandon the steering wheel, and leave your car in the middle of the crossroads. In the city one may find oneself in a traffic jam in a part of Via Maqueda that is officially closed to traffic. In the city you may find yourself having to make a right turn, only to find yourself in a back street with a street market ahead of you, and no way out. The traffic bylaws ensure that in a situation like this all you can do is turn off the motor and wait for nightfall, when the market stalls are dismantled and it is possible to drive through again.

True, these are small glitches in traffic regulation, quickly rectified in a matter of days, and this is a comfort. It proves that there exists an expert or consultant who keeps an eye on the traffic and does the necessary. Or perhaps we're looking at a panel of experts in continual consultation so as to achieve the best results for the motorist. Only the awareness that some inscrutable master plan exists makes one accept the fact that each time, invariably, the cure is worse than the disease, the patch worse than the hole.

Motorists are not even granted the assurance that if the traffic is crazy, at least its craziness has its own stability and may be relied upon, so one may take one's dispositions on a daily basis, and be acquainted with the small compromises one may get away with. Today we may, with reasonable assurance of impunity, slip through the one-way street the wrong way, the one linking Via Pandolfini with Viale Lazio – it's only short, and takes us through the petrol station; but tomorrow, who knows? And all those zones 'for restricted traffic', in the absence of further specifications, exactly who is restricted from entering? Seemingly everyone drives through, can't I do so too without penalty?

It is significant to observe that a brief, intense rage rubs shoulders with a quiet resignation. The light turns green, and all is forgiven. The fleeting rage of the motorist is the most surprising of symptoms. In the look of those stuck in the traffic jam there is a straw fire, but in fact every plan to organize the traffic, however absurd, is greeted with general indifference. Each punitive regulation is metabolized as something ineluctable. The motorist's resignation is founded upon a narcotic nostalgia that we nurture for past times and yesterday's traffic: when there were cycle lanes in Via Libertà. They were discontinued because they prevented drivers parking on the kerb. But it's point-less to hanker after olden times, not least because, even allowing for the softer focus of the passage of time, it was still appalling traffic even back then, and cycle paths in Via Libertà were a joke, seeing that they were interrupted by projecting stalls of one kind and another all the way along. But at least they were remedies to the traffic of our younger days. And during our younger days, how happy we all were!

It needs also to be said that, aside from this sort of nos-talgic languor, the memory of the city-dwellers functions spasmodically. There are often short circuits between short-term and long-term memory. Occasionally events of recent date are forgotten even when they stirred up extreme indignation. Probably the city-dwellers possess somewhere in their mental circuits a reset button. A button they inadvertently press before each election that wipes the hard drive clean. That's the only way to explain the fact that never in their memory does any trace subsist of promises made and the ensuing disappointment; only in that way can one explain the blithe masochism that forever characterizes the city-dweller on his way to the polling station.

For completeness sake the reset button is pressed once again after leaving the polling station, which is why the locals almost never remember who it was they voted for last time and why they feel entirely in their right to grumble every time a given quarter misses its turn for the water distribution. And this is why in bars, shops and porters' lodges the chorus of indignation over unemployment is a veritable blizzard – and the indignation is bloodthirsty enough as if any day now it will find its outlet in a new Sicilian Vespers.

We must not forget, though, that the Sicilian Vespers was occasioned not by one of the countless irritations suffered by the inhabitants over the centuries, but by a single insult addressed to the honour of a lady. The French oppressed, bullied, harassed just as before and after them the Phoenicians, Greeks, Romans, Byzantines, Arabs, Normans, Swabians, Aragonese, Bourbons, Savoy and you-name-it. But the event that blew the fuse of resignation so violently was one word too many addressed to a lady. This should make one reflect on the scale of values governing the wrath of the city's inhabitants.

When there is a water shortage, and when the contract is not renewed for one of the many unions of casual workers, at once you have road blocks, with an excess of collective rage that is positively frightening: crates are set ablaze, cars overturned, buses halted with burst tyres, insults hurled at the authorities – enough to leave one thinking that the collective conscience has been stirred and never, but never again shall the citizens lie down under the systematic betrayal of promises. You, naive traveller that you are, imagine that at the next elections these hotheads will teach a lesson to the politicians who have so wickedly deceived them. They will finally remember that the people appointed to sort out the failings in the water supply and in the labour market are the same lot who created the problems in the first place. The proverb says: 'No one is so ignorant as not to know whether the shoe fits'. But your political consciousness is out of order: that's not how it will be, because the city-dwellers are unable to make the connection between today's election and yesterday's or tomorrow's. Because, alas, somebody will always press reset, the memory is wiped clean, and the elections will turn out just as they always have.

4

Death is not as bad as they make it out to be

Reading back what's been written so far, I realize that in my efforts to persuade you to overcome your fears all I have done is stir them up. And I'm afraid that this chapter, too, will not help you find the will to step out of your room. Rather, prepare yourself, because now I am going to try to explain how the city-dwellers view death. You are at liberty to cross your fingers as much as you like, but you've got to know about this as well.

If you have a friend in the city, you will already have arranged to meet this person for a conducted tour. He may even be awaiting your phone call to come round and collect you. And you in the meantime have had second thoughts. You must telephone to cancel the appointment or at least to postpone it. It will not be easy, though, to explain to him why you don't feel ready. All he wants is to be kind and hospitable, taking you to see the high spots – Piazza Pretoria, the cathedral, Palazzo dei Normanni – but fitting in on the way, along with the beautiful monuments, those street corners where the most notorious Mafia outrages have been committed. This is where General Dalla Chiesa was killed, here is where Pio La Torre was gunned down, and so forth.

A veritable, albeit illusionary, tour of the murder sites was organized some years ago by a tour agent – this gave him access, in the guise of scandalized polemics, to all the publicity he wanted. The tour was organized but never took place. However, the circuit by car which the city-dwellers keep up their sleeve for first-time visitors is precisely the same thing: a circuit that gives a good example of the offhand approach with which they face up to death. Typical is the sorrow (false) and irony (genuine) with which they exhibit to the visitor the places where the Mafia carried out a killing: 'Here's where they shot Gaetano Costa, poor thing.'

Where the term 'poor thing' stands for the sorrow that the crime still provokes so many years later. In actual fact, while the guide is pointing out the spot on the pavement in Via Cavour he is scrutinizing the visitor's face to see how he reacts: is there any reaction, and if so, what sort? Trying to ascertain how far one might be able to press this funerary re-evocation, and whether the traveller is up to following the argument. Is his relationship with death sufficiently ironic and resilient enough for him to be accepted into the city-dwellers' community?

Another example of this rapport the city-dweller has with death is the way he changes over time in his attitude to children. The dead come to visit the city children at regularly intervals. For the children it is a terrifying night, the same one each year. The night between 1 and 2 November. There is nothing unexpected about it: it is known in advance, is discussed for days on end, and becomes only the more worrying. The worry, and also the anticipation, because the dead come with gifts. That is how the city-dwellers celebrate All Souls' Day: the elderly deceased come bearing gifts for the young living. In these latitudes the Epiphany witch, the Befana, has never taken hold, and even Father Christmas has a job competing with a host of deceased relatives who return to stir the recollections within the bosom of their own ex-families.

The parents act as intermediaries, because while it is certainly the deceased who bring the presents, they first have to sort out certain agreements with Mum and Dad on the tricks to be played. Once these have been agreed, there still remains the matter of the ultimate test of bravery to be surmounted. On the evening of 1 November, the children go to bed in a panic and can't get to sleep; and the longer it takes them to get off to sleep, the worse the panic becomes. There is equal obstinacy on either side, and yet the total opposite to that of every other night of the year, when the object is to put off closing one's eyes for as long as possible. The night between 1 and 2 November is the exception, one has to get off to sleep as quickly as possible. One cooks up yawns well ahead of bedtime in order to be put to bed there and then. And of course, once under the blankets, that's it – sleep just doesn't come. It's like watching the saucepan, waiting for the water to start boiling: according to an island proverb, you have only to keep looking and you keep it from boiling.

For the child the problem is to get off to sleep before the dead arrive. This proves impossible because during all the vacillation between waking and sleeping they are assailed by thoughts such as: what will they be like, these dead folk, bless 'em? Will they be as they were when still alive, maybe just a touch paler, or will they be wrapped in a shroud? Or will they be all too realistically corpse-like? In the event, those who have been dead a long time will probably be skeletons. But Grandad who died last year will surely have the odd bit of putrefied flesh still attached to his bones. If he finds me awake, that will be embarrassing. I'll have to hug him and kiss him, that sort of thing. Why can't I get to sleep?

In the worst case, the child muses, if Grandad comes and I'm still awake, I can always pretend to be asleep. Keep my eyes shut. But will I be able to resist the temptation to open them for a split second, just to see how he's changed in the meantime? And what if he notices that I'm only pretending to be asleep? The dead are wise to these things. Won't I look a proper Charley?

The grown-ups have put him to bed with a smile. For them it's a small matter – just wait, tonight Grandad is going to bring you a lovely present. But it's an ineffective smile, it is one of those that come just before an injection. They smile, but what do they care? They conceal the real problem of what's happened to Grandad in the meantime.

The laceration derives from the fact that the children of today belong to an intermediate generation, caught between the tradition of All Souls' and the forced march to modernity that comes with television. The grown-ups talk blithely of the dead, and the children imagine one of those zombies they've seen on the screen. Today's children have no luck: they are stuck midway between two cultures. For them the dead are at the same time a cheerful thought and one hell of a worry. Who's right? Mum and Dad or the television? Out of this split mind comes the anxious elation that possesses them on that night.

Sleep does, however, always come, and almost never a sleep populated with nightmares: it is a peaceful sleep. And in the morning there is somewhere or other a hidden present to go looking for. The present is a relief, of course, but who was it who brought it? Grandad, or a carcase seething with worms? Or was it one's parents, as some wide boy among one's friends already supposes, the rotter!

On second thoughts, looking at it from a grown-up's standpoint, the whole idea of All Souls' Day is out of keeping with the Western culture of mourning. What is there to celebrate about death? What joy is to be obtained from commemorating the deceased? And yet that's what happens in the city. Perhaps a cult of the dead as coherent as this will find its echo only among the people of Mexico. Or in the familiarity with which 700,000 people in Cairo make their homes in the cemeteries.

Recent bereavements of those close to us are always demonstrated ostentatiously and tragically, like local newspaper headlines. But once the grieving is less stringent, a vein of black humour comes to the surface. Jokes are made about the dead in order to exorcize death itself. Not for nothing does the patron saint of the city, Rosalia, hold a skull in her hand, an authentic memento mori for all the faithful. Not for nothing is the catacomb of the Capuchins one of the stops on the canonical tour that the city-dwellers inflict upon the traveller with the aim of scaring him.

Until the last century it could happen that once you were dead you were hung on the wall, like a picture. There are hundreds of corpses still thus exposed in the catacomb of the Capuchins, where foreign visitors are always taken for the pure and simple pleasure of getting a rise out of them.

A form of black humour that comes close to sadism still obtains in gastronomic circles, when visitors are taken to try out certain specialities like *musso*, *frittola*, *stigghiòla*, *milza*. These are various kinds of offal, bits that are normally discarded. They are not really meat, but the ghost of meat, cooked in frightening amounts of fat, the very carnival of dead meat. What attracts and repulses the traveller in the street markets is the sight of kid goats' heads, of little animals stripped of their skin and hung up, of necklaces of cows' tongues exhibited as signs outside butchers' shops. Indeed, they are *Carnazzerie*, the term used in these parts.

It is a sadistic pleasure typical of the islander, and is to be met with even in Lampedusa's novel, *The Leopard*, when the younger nephew of the Prince goes out of his way to describe to the Piedmontese Chevalley the ordeals which the island's brigands were accustomed to make their kidnapped prisoners undergo – preferably prisoners from the mainland, like Chevalley himself – if the family took their time over producing the ransom. In the catacomb of the Capuchins, too, dead meat is displayed grotesquely and theatrically. The place would be terrifying were the display not so brazen. Besides, the sheer quantity serves to weaken the dramatic effect. To stumble across a mummy could send one into a panic, but a whole stream of mummies smacks rather of the carnival.

Below ground there are long corridors, and on the walls of the corridors, the corpses. They are definitely more corpse-like than mummies, being bodies that have just been summarily preserved. The drying rooms are still retained, where the corpses were left to be purged any old how. Once they were little more than skeletons, they were reclothed and hung up on this wall and that, classified in accordance with their social status. One wall for the middle class, one for the aristocracy, one for prelates, one for children, all of them wearing the clothes they had when still living. So as not to leave the smallest chink of wall vacant, they each had their coffin left at their feet.

Then it would happen that on All Souls' Day or on the anniversary of the departed one's death, the family would come to pay a visit to the good soul. They would turn up at the Capuchins in as complete a family delegation as possible. On ordinary days there were chairs set out, but on 2 November, given the swarm of visitors, it was wiser to bring one's own from home if one wanted to be comfortable. With the dead, in fact, it was customary to make a salon. The chairs would be set down at the corpse's feet and conversation would begin. The favourite topic was everything that had happened in the year since the last visit: 'Ninetta got married, Calogero had a little boy, the neighbours emigrated, Uncle died ...'

A monologue conducted by the living, and it could go on half the day. There would be moments of embarrassment, as always happens when one of the participants has nothing to say. With this in mind it was usual to bring some refreshment from home. Everyone ate and drank and chatted away until it was time to conclude the visit and leave.

An analogous version of the visit to the dead continues to take place to this day, when nobody is any longer hung up on the walls of the Capuchins. On 2 November the surviving members of the family go to the cemetery and take their places round the grave. The one real difference is in the position of the deceased, who is horizontal and invisible, present only beneath the intervening marble slab. However, the topics of conversation and the state of mind of the family are much the same; except in the case of recent bereavements and instances of particular devotion, the tone is kept light. The deceased was and remains one of the family, to be put at ease as much as possible. Very much so: you mustn't depress him with gloomy talk, seeing that he is obliged to spend his time in such a gloomy place. The family feel obliged to cheer him up, if only once a year.

As in Macondo, the village dreamed up by García Márquez, in the city the dead are only dead up to a point. They interact with the living, they are on hand when needed to dispense sage advice. They interact with the living family inasmuch as they have all the better title and experience to put in their own two pennyworth. Contacts are also maintained through the dying: Leonardo

Sciascia used to tell of an elderly relative on his deathbed, and family and friends, knowing this was the case, crowding round his bed and quite unblushingly urging him to convey their greetings to deceased loved ones. After umpteen of these requests, the dying man made a gesture of despair: 'Be kind, and write all this down for me on a sheet of paper, otherwise I'm going to forget.'

Death is a joking matter. There is laughter so as to avoid tears. The majority of ghosts and spectres that haunt the land in the legends are benign spirits; the only ones evilly disposed towards the living are those who died by violence. Like the brigands mentioned by the nephew in *The Leopard*, and like the preserved corpses among the Capuchins, the spirits that enliven places and buildings are more there to be *utilized* by the living to scare others than to be frightening in or of themselves. They are, of their nature, decidedly tame.

There is, for example, the young nun who inhabits the Teatro Massimo. According to tradition, her soul has been in torment ever since the convent that had been there, and the church of San Giuliano, were torn down in order to build the Teatro, and the centuries-old graveyard was dug up. There are accounts of her various enigmatic apparitions to the theatre staff. She does nothing in particular: just appears, disappears, that's it.

But it would be wrong to suppose that the rapport with death is static. No, it is subject to constant transformations. Even All Souls' Day, especially in the upper levels of society, no longer exercises the same fascination it did 20 years ago. Even for the children of the city death is becoming a premature problem. This is the result of a cultural shift, now that the middle classes have progressively abandoned the tradition of bringing gifts to the dead; they prefer to import the celebration of Hallowe'en which, next to the commemoration of the dead in the city, looks like a childish bit of foolery. The All Souls' tradition now only survives among the working classes, and who knows how long it will continue even there? It is a cultural and maybe even a genetic shift. To begin with, one had to reckon early with death; at three years old one was old enough to know one had to die, sooner or later, and thus come to terms with death.

You too, traveller, given that you are now in the city, try to enter into the spirit of the place with all the sense of humour you can muster on topics of this kind. Take a deep breath, cross your fingers or whatever. Bear in mind that in this department too something is changing, the modern world is encroaching. But it's taking its time.

5

Faces and expressions

Another thing that's changing, for example, is the technique of facial expressions. This is another thing you need to be warned about. Not to alarm you, nor to reassure you too much. Forewarn you, though, yes. Before you decide once and for all to leave your hotel, you have to know that there is a look which women travellers in particular are inclined to misinterpret. They already start to misinterpret it on the ferry taking them from Scylla to Charybdis, when they notice a change in the way men look at them, the way it becomes more intrusive. These are insistent, lecherous looks that make a woman feel ill at ease. It is a feeling that comes to be considered among the most uncomfortable characteristics of the islanders. When speaking of the look on the faces of male islanders, the comments are never flattering. At best the annoyance comes to be tempered by a series of unflattering expressions. True, that look is vulgar, but that is your islander for you. Enough 'even so's, a whole lot of things on the island are shrugged off.

The looks which are so irritating are those termed by Vitaliano Brancati as *ingravidabalconi*, in other words, they mean to penetrate the shutters of houses in order to imagine the secret life going on behind them.

Nevertheless, the woman traveller gets it wrong if she thinks that the lustful look might be the prelude to physical molestation. This happens only sporadically; womankind is generally kept on the altar of untouchability. If you, reader, are a woman traveller and thus hesitating to confront the city, think again. There are no statistics, but on the island bodily violence does not readily translate into social, group violence; there is the occasional rape, the work of an unbalanced person, the traditional equilibrium being thrown off-balance owing to contamination by the modern world. Not the same thing as openly admitted crimes, often of great violence; but in the Mafia code, violence against women and children is severely punished. And however repulsive, the Mafia code remains a sure thermometer for taking the cultural temperature.

But of course the distaste that comes from seeing oneself under insistent observation goes beyond the fear of physical assault. The accepted view anywhere else in the world encourages us to regard our private sphere as proof against other people's stares. How dare they! And up to a point they are right: how dare they? Every glance is an assessment, and everyone has the right not to undergo, not to feel themselves, being assessed. The looks that you noticed before you shut yourself up in your hotel seemed intent on weighing you up body and soul.

Here is the misapprehension. The owner of the lustful look might excuse himself in a paraphrase of Signora Morte's words in Vecchioni's *Samarcanda*:

... You are wrong, soldier, you deceive yourself:
There was no mischief in my look.
It was merely a look of astonishment ...

And so on. But here is the point: the look of astonishment. The capacity to maintain over the centuries
this technique of a look charged with astonishment does
make the experience of seduction on the island virtually
unique in anthropology. As occurs in Arab countries, any
question of chastity of comportment is accorded to the
eyes – the only part of the body left exposed, the only
part to which the language of seduction is entrusted. And
even today, when a larger area of the body is exposed, the
eyes of the city look in the same way.

... I was expecting you today at Samarcanda,
What were you doing there two days ago?

The look expresses the false dismay at running into
one's destiny right there, right at that moment. Nothing
odd about that. Whoever looks, treads that path the
whole time. But the capacity to be astonished by so little
is a way to keep the eyes constantly exercized.

Besides, every misunderstanding by a woman ought to
be set by the consideration that nowadays women, girls
no matter how young, are pretty much equally inclined
to stare. They too charge their look with the suggestion
of seduction. And we're not talking merely about hidden,
fleeting glances from down up. Quite the opposite: the
looks cast by the women of the city are often direct,

unabashed, openly provocative and not lacking the shade of ambiguity. In actual fact, the women's glances, if you know how to intercept them, are no less intrusive than those of the men. The game provides for a reciprocity, and maybe this feminine enterprise is not even to be ascribed to a conquest of emancipation. Already, back in the sixteenth century, a traveller like Brydone had described the sensuality of the soirées in Piazza Marina. A small orchestra played in the total darkness. The city Fathers avoided providing public lighting, the darkness was there on purpose to allow ladies and gentlemen to canoodle as discreetly as possible. Brydone hints that in the obscurity of Piazza Marina any suggestion of putative chastity among the city-dwellers was roundly disproved.

True, traditionally the role of reflex seduction was reserved for women. Given the small number of opportunities, to meet a woman's glance was, for a long time, a highly charged affair. The same love-play obtains even today, when the rules have ostensibly changed, as has the topography of seduction. But even today seductions take place in the natural order of things, when out for a stroll. It's the same thing for the timings: Saturday and Sunday are the days for seduction. Lower-middle-class youth find their principal outlet for seduction on the traffic island in the middle of Via Belmonte, or in Piazza Politeama, of an afternoon, when groups of young people go courting in accordance with traditional methods. Only feminine glances have changed – along with girls' smiles and their attire – from what they once were. Two boys strike up a conversation with two girls under some pretext. The girls don't look at them and keep silent, they just keep strolling. But the boys persist, and it's obvious enough that the girls aren't heading for anywhere in particular, they are there for the same reason as the boys, in order to please and entice. Or else to recite the verb 'to look' in its threefold dialect incarnation: *taliàre, mommiàre, allucàre*. Three verbs to say the same thing, that is, not only to look, but specifically to look with dizzy lust. *Talè como talia*. Look at how she's looking at you.

Higher up the social scale, courting takes place in an altogether more rarefied manner. But here too the look, be it male or female, is a vital component, if only in the specific form of the *occhio del mondo*: people are watching, therefore we have to lay on the charade of seduction. It is almost a social obligation. Even if it is only to disguise the erotic attraction, the most enticing of scenarios, but we mustn't be too obvious about it.

At parties and in clubs, the self-respecting bourgeoisie rub shoulders with the aristocracy, both of them flaunting excess and backbiting. Backbiting about excess. The over-excitement of the young and the impotence of their elders turn into verbal sallies and the peddling of scandal. People still talk of the shy journalist who took off her shoes and danced on the table-top. Or of Baron La Lomia who, in the course of his studies, identified 34 types of woman to be found in the natural order, each one distinct by character and sexual preference.

Today, as yesterday, the majority of the true-blue aristocracy of the city considers the idea of work an offence against its status. Hence it has the time and opportunity to cultivate its extravagances even in amorous matters. We're talking about a kind of collector's bug by way of entertainment, often no more than an end in itself. Compared with elsewhere, in this context seduction is an entirely abstract game, next to which a game of chess is ruthlessly down to earth. In the game of love the parties require that when they catch each other's eye very often little or nothing ensues. There is even a name for those girls who incline more to courtship than to con-summation: 'perfumers', in the sense that they give top priority to the sense of smell, which outranks sight and even more touch. They permit their scent to be picked up, and they may even use their eyes, but they do not touch nor allow themselves to be touched. And yet ful-filment subsists equally and coincides with the pleasure of the game itself. Sex is important, of course it is, but it remains a secondary detail. Just as in chess, the player who sees he has lost knocks down the king before arriv-ing at the explicit humiliation of checkmate, in the same way the perversity of the islander prefers to stop short by a second or two, skipping at that point the banality of consummated sex.

All these fine discourses would not be worth a damn if they did not proceed from the presupposition that, in the city, looks have something about them that you do not find in looks anywhere else. At a pinch they may come close to looks that are native to southern European countries. South here could mean equally well the East as the West, so long as it features as a periphery to the great capitals and the great capital. Looks on the world's peripheries have this in particular about them: they exist, and must be taken into account.

Suppose a lady gets into a carriage on the Paris Métro. She is holding a wilted daisy. As wilted as could be. Virtually without a single petal. The lady also has a series of nervous tics, mutters to herself, and shows every sign of madness. Her presence on any public transport in the city would give rise to a spread of reactions ranging from disdain to pity; not so in the Paris Métro. Useless to look for such reactions in the eyes of the couple of dozen people in the same carriage: no sign of them. Useless to look for other reactions: there are none. No reaction. They've simply not noticed. It's not as if they're pretending not to notice: they genuinely don't notice. For the significant sampling of the population of any and every class and race there at that moment, the lady with the wilted flower does not exist. As if she had not entered into their field of vision. Of course the lady can in this way go about her business without attracting the morbid attention of the bystanders, but is this in fact all to the good? Does toleration in fact coincide with invisibility?

From this point of view, in the city – city in a manner of speaking, seeing that it subsists on the edge of provinciality – looks are a guarantee of a person's actually being in existence. Because here there exists at least the remote possibility of meeting an acquaintance when you happen upon a person. In the provinces one looks at a person to establish whether you are acquainted. Of course often this is not the case, but a look, if only just one glance, is anybody's right. The first look is, at all events, a contact from which may follow a thousand effects, or none. But there it is, in the meantime. And two looks which intersect never fail to exact a mutual promise to tell the stories they have to tell. In a metropolis, on the other hand, looks glance over one another and never catch the other's eye. It is difficult to suppose that you'll know a person you happen upon, so what's the point of looking at the person? So looking at people is needless. So no looking. Never.

In the city looks always express a lack of indifference, and this may be ferocity or gentleness, as the case may be. But looks always have something to express. The difficulty lies in having to subject all of this theory of looks to the scrutiny of somebody arriving from the north, from the centre, or from one of the capitals. One of the inconveniences of living *in partibus infidelium* is being resigned to having to attend to the inflow of press correspondents. In the city the special correspondents of the leading papers generally arrive in the immediate aftermath of an assassination or just ahead of local elections. Or indeed when they are sent to report on a supposed renaissance or a supposed sign of decay. The correspondent arrives, sniffs about, does his rounds, collects a number of quotable impressions, goes home and concludes the task for which he has been sent. The article then gets to be read in the city with a mixture of trepidation (first) and disappointment (later). Trepidation along the lines of, 'Let's see what the man has written this time' and disappointment along the lines of, 'Well, the fact is we're a whole lot more complex than that'.

The city-dwellers fancy themselves extremely complex. They take offence at any simplification regarding themselves. There exists a kind of embarrassed susceptibility that the islanders have in common with the Jews, both of them peoples who have turned guilty feelings into an inherent trait of character. On further thought, however, the islanders know perfectly well to what they owe their guilt complex: they believe they are debtors to the world at large because it is from their island that the Mafia has spread throughout the world and soiled it. The islanders, even the honest ones, believe in the depth of their hearts that they belong to a tribe of plague-spreaders. They are even quite ready to admit it, indeed they are the first to cast aspersions on their city, just as the Jews talk themselves down. At the same time, though – once again, like the Jews – they won't have other people disparaging them. Though they don't place themselves up on the same level as the rest of the world, they look down on the world. Some of them do this on purpose. Bear this in mind should you find yourself launched on the *mare magnum* of a discussion with a local. He will probably start by running down his city. He'll trash it. But take care: it is a trap. Should you make the mistake of agreeing with the opinions flaunted by your interlocutor, you're done for. If you say, yes, the city is quite as bad as you make it out, he'll turn his back on you once and for all. You must appear to disagree with him. Tell him he mustn't exaggerate, the city strikes you as a marvellous place. This is the response he is expecting from you. On this script the interplay requires you to take issue with him.

The understanding is that outsiders are incapable of grasping certain subtleties. Like the Jews, the islanders cultivate the general conviction that their civilization is more complicated than any other. It may be better, it may be worse, but it is certainly more complex and radical. In point of fact they're not more complicated, they only *think* they are. Which complicates matters. And this is our starting point.

To avoid complications, among the inconveniences of living *in partibus infidelium*, there is sometimes the requirement to escort one of these journalists as he does his rounds of the city. The courtesy is a by-product that abuts on the hope of damage-limitation. It may happen that one escorts the reporter from one of the top weeklies, *Espresso* or *Panorama* (the weeklies *in partibus infidelium*, however unlike each other, tend to look alike), who has to write an article on the so-called *movida* (social relocation) in the city. In such a case, we have to take him to some fashionable spot, one frequented by the last couple of generations of the bourgeoisie, where they go to spot each other.

Between one aperitif and the next it is more than likely that the conversation will come round to looking at the faces of the people present. It will be easy for the correspondent to note that the faces all look very much alike, almost indistinguishable from their peers in Parioli or San Babila. Good work – the gleam in his eye signals that the correspondent has lit upon his story, and from this point on it will be impossible to prise him away from it. Besides, it is true to say that it does make a story. The faces have changed, and continue to change. The classic physiognomy of the elderly with their sculpted faces is disappearing – faces that naturally express the weight of centuries of being the underdog added to those still to be endured. In all the myriad of places open to the public which give the idea of social vivacity, this is the face one is most likely to meet, a face on which a suntan rubs shoulders light-heartedly with skin cancer.

No point trying to explain to the correspondent that, rather than an improvement, this represents the actual problem. If the faces of the young in the city look similar to those in Rome or Milan, that means that something serious is happening in a field comprising genetics and anthropology. If it is in fact to be doubted whether looking like someone else, and not least like certain other persons, is a good thing, it is certainly not gratifying to arrive at such a resemblance some years behind the prescribed model. Herein lies the essence of provincialism: to achieve a style outside the prescribed time limits. Is the existential and cultural model prevailing today throughout the nation a desirable one? Should we be conforming our features to this existential and cultural model? And what is the sense of doing so when the model is now passé?

Looks are important, faces are important. The faces in the city have stories to tell that are completely different from those told by faces in any other city in the world. Not necessarily better, not necessarily worse: just different. The assimilation of faces and looks is a risk that the city is running, but no one is saying it is the price to be paid for keeping up to date. In fact the challenge, to be above board, has to be in keeping with the island's tradition of sociability.

Take an example: in just a few years three McDonald's have opened. The McDonald's are always an interesting indication of joining the world mainstream. Within a certain band of underdevelopment, they are even a consolation: they warrant that an international standard of security and stability has been achieved. Above a certain degree of development, however, they give cause for concern. The branches in the city are always crowded, nor is it difficult to imagine that other branches will be opened before long. Now, the ideal solution would be to open a McDonald's giving each customer the choice between a cheeseburger and *pane e panelle* – the local round loaf. As a matter of fact in both cases we are talking about fast food, and for the customer the cholesterol count will be more or less the same either way. Naturally this is but a pious illusion, because with a cheeseburger and *pane e panelle* one of the two contenders is set up as a foreign invader while the other is totally innocent of this, so in the long run the one is bound to get the upper hand.

This is the slippery slope on which the city finds herself; you see it reflected in the faces and looks of her inhabitants. Especially in those of the young and of children. One tries to explain these subtleties to the correspondent, whether he is from *Espresso* or *Panorama*, and eventually the correspondent seems to be persuaded. He certainly looks it. Then, once he's back home, he spreads himself over five columns, the gist of which is, more or less: 'Great! How very modern! The faces of the youth of the city look just like those in Milan.'

6

To do with eating

All that has been said so far has been based on the supposition that love and death, looks and facial expressions form part of a city's landscape. But before arriving at the urban structure and the monuments themselves, there are many other components to a city's landscape: smells and flavours, for example. One may go to museums, true enough. And visit churches. But to get some idea of the city you have to go to one of the street markets, or even only to a fry-up shop.

This rule applies to every town in the world, but all the more so here, given that the city tends to offer a singularly aromatic and flavoursome image of itself. Indeed the city takes pride in this succulence. This is the version it wants to publicize. But there are smells and flavours that will remain unknown to you, unless you manage to enter into the bosom of a family who invites you to lunch. Such a lunch invitation is to be prized. Only in a private house can you get any idea of such delicacies as fried whitebait, which restaurants don't offer – or it least, aren't supposed to – because there's a ban on fishing for newly spawned fish. Only in this way can you acquaint yourself with the dish which, by its form and substance, represents the totem of domestic gastronomy: *brociolone*. No point looking through cookbooks for the right way to prepare *brociolone* – you won't find it there. It is by and large a big meatball, but there is no real recipe for it because each housewife makes it as she fancies and with the ingredients she has to hand. We may be looking at a single slice of meat or at a wodge of mincemeat, as the case may be. The stuffing is composed of certain standard ingredients, though even these change from one household to the next depending on what leftovers there are from previous days: hard-boiled eggs, cheese, ham, etc. Even the accompanying vegetables change from one moment to the next; the principal variants are peas, potatoes or tomato sauce. Like the *brociolone*, pasta with broccoli in a pan is a family favourite, as is pasta with sardines, pasta with anchovy and toasted breadcrumbs, tuna in sauce, and even the bean fritters which may be found only now and again in a restaurant.

Vast also is the repertoire of public flavours, and in each one of them you may recognize a characteristic that identifies the city. You go out, maybe only for a coffee. Perhaps this is all it will take to break the spell that is holding you back. You know that in the south of Italy coffee is considered just the thing to break the ice. Coffee belongs to a highly significant classification: here the café culture exists, but it differs vastly from that to be found in Naples – in Naples, coffee-drinking is a happily extrovert ceremony, while in the city it features as a ritual act of contrition. In these parts coffee is taken as a necessity, and even if it is actually a coffee break, we are talking about a crucial one. We say: 'I have to have a coffee.' This expression reflects the element of compulsion undergone: coffee may be compared with the vital fix needed by a drug addict. This distinction is a peculiarity, and helps to underscore the difference between the two cities which are often, wrongly, lumped together. In point of fact, to the same measure that Naples is extrovert, the city is introvert. Take an example: in the city's churches one prays – or rather, in most cases, it is the women who do the praying, as the men only go to church on Sundays – almost bent over double, in a posture which is itself an act of expiation. In Naples, however, men and women kneel (or stand) composedly in front of the statues of saints, and above all with their arms flung open and their hands palm upward, as though to act as aerials with as much of their body surface as possible so as to obtain the best possible infusion of Divine Grace.

To return to the bar, you have to know that in the city coffee is normally served *ristretto* – at double strength; the quantity in the coffee cup should be no more than a finger's breadth, better still that of the little finger. Unless the customer specifies otherwise, and often even if he does specify otherwise, what is set down on the counter is a concentrate of adrenaline. The canonical double-strength does not prevent the customer from indulging in personal requests. The coffee may in fact be: double-strength plus (!), *lungo* (thinned out), hot, cold, cold granulated, cold without sugar, *corretto* (laced with grappa), *macchiato* (with a dash of milk), *macchiato* hot, *macchiato* cold, *macchiato* with milk served separately, decaffeinated, with sweetener, with cane sugar, cappuccino, cappuccino with the coffee served separately, hot *caffelatte*, cold *caffelatte*, in a large cup, in a plastic cup, in a bottle to take out ready-sugared, in a bottle to take out sugarless, and a whole lot of other variants ad lib. As Enzensberger has already noted, this apparent freedom of choice, which is typically Italian, corresponds with a substantial uniformity of taste. In other words, the barman will in every case serve what suits him best in the matter of temperature, quantity and flavour, without reference to customers' orders.

Every city-dweller has his favourite kind of coffee, and his favourite café where they make it the way he, and only he, likes it. This pretension towards originality has a very varied phenomenology. One distinctive characteristic, for instance, consists of the requirement to change the names of things and places in order to make them conform to one's own fancy. We have already mentioned Santa Maria dei Naufragati (St Mary of the Shipwrecked) which has been turned into Annegati (of the Drowned). Here is another example: St Augustine is not considered an adequate patron saint for the beautiful church in the Capo quarter, and the locals have used their own discretion to rechristen it Santa Rita. It is a tendency towards personalization that offers many examples in the city's place names: the piazza generally referred to as Piazza Politeama actually comprises two distinct ones, contiguous and unacknowledged – Piazza Castelnuovo and Piazza Ruggiero Settimo; Piazza Mordini becomes Piazza Croci; Piazza Verdi is generally known as Piazza Massimo; Piazza Giulio Cesare is simply The Station, without a Piazza; likewise Piazza Vittorio Veneto has become simply The Statue. Hence we find dialogues which may seem quite surreal to an outsider: 'Where d'you live?' 'At The Statue.' Where, in any case, the statue of Victory is practically invisible, perched as it is atop an obelisk. But for the city-dwellers, changing the name of something signifies adapting it to one's own fancy and thus asserting one's own personality. Notwithstanding the fact that everything remains exactly as it always was. Precisely like the coffee.

As a general rule the coffee is served in little cups and almost scalding. In order to certainly achieve the object of burning the customer's lips, the cup is kept on top of the espresso machine and left to achieve a high temperature. Only after a couple of hours can the cup be considered ready for use. After the initial shock, the customer may ask for the cup to be changed, and the barman may or may not do as asked, with good or evil grace. If he does so, holding the cup beneath the cold tap, the barman will nonetheless maintain an Olympian attitude, as much as to say: 'The things they make me do!' At all events that customer will, from that moment, be beneath his notice. Which is a reason why the customer, rather than forfeit the respect of the barman, will not protest but will hang on to the red-hot coffee cup. For this reason, and also because the red-hot cup symbolizes a certain sado-masochism that distinguishes the city-dwellers in their personal relationships, and in their relationship with outsiders.

Another aromatic classification is well represented by *stigghiòla*. *Stigghiòla* (invariably feminine plural) is intestine of lamb or calf cleaned out any old how and restuffed.

The variant using goat is a refinement. *Stigghiòla* is for sale off certain barrows at strategic points throughout the city, always on the pavement, and in questionable hygienic conditions. Moreover, the cognoscenti prize the flavour of the confection above its sanitary wholesomeness – indeed some would in this case consider the latter counterproductive. It is as well to distrust a person who is ready to put his hand in the fire to commend a given vendor of the product. The barrows specializing in *stigghiòla* signal their presence with the odoriferous cloud surrounding them, and with the small compact crowd of idlers shuffling around them. The customer who is not a regular, if he wants to safeguard his digestive tract, will do well to have himself introduced, or to have on him some sort of credentials: 'I've been sent by Uncle So-and-So, etc.' No need for Uncle So-and-So even to know that his name has been mentioned. No need for Uncle So-and-So even to be a real person.

Stigghiòla represents the apex of a roadside gastronomy that also includes the *musso*, *quarume* and *frittola*. *Musso* and *quarume* are the boiled ears, snout and entrails of veal. The *frittola* is kept in a lined basket and covered with a cloth to maintain its temperature. If asked, the hawker will dip his hand into the container and pull out a fistful of greasy-looking bits and pieces, offering them on a piece of greaseproof paper. Of what these bits and pieces consist is anyone's guess, and the cloth helps to preserve the mystery. The theory is that they represent beef and pig gristle that has been boiled up, then fried and sprinkled with saffron.

There is more than meets the eye to the barrows selling these products – they are also test-beds. The city-dwellers will bring you here to put your stomach and your courage to the test. The offer of *frittola* may be compared to the tour of murder victims to which visitors are exposed in order to get an idea of their endurance. One and the same is the spirit in which the suggestion of *frittola* is made and the shudder which in most cases this occasions. We do not know precisely why a city that is otherwise so welcoming makes her guests undergo this treatment. What is certain is that the city-dwellers derive a sort of morose amusement from these sadistic exercises.

Alongside *stigghiola*, *musso* and *frittola*, bread with *milza* (animal spleen) represents a gastronomic evolution, the link in the chain leading to *pane e panelle*. In the fried food shops, the *milza* is cooked in lard and kept hot in a pan which mostly contains lung fragments. *Focaccia* with *milza* is subdivided into *schiette* (plain) and *maritate* (married), the latter complete with grated cheese and ricotta. A recent optional extra is lemon. In this case especially, for better service, the thing is to know or be known to the cook, so that he will fish out of the pot pieces considered to be more choice or not so tough. One sight of anthropological interest may be observed at the *rosticceria* at Porta Carbone in the early hours of the morning, when there is a small traffic jam of cars and particularly lorries. A ritual requires that before setting out on his daily round, the lorry driver partakes of a *panino* with *milza*. Given the hour, we are looking at a test of courage somewhere between flirting with the Evil Eye and flaunting one's machismo.

Coming to *panelle*, which are fritters using ground chickpeas, we confront a phenomenon not unlike that already observed with the scalding cup of coffee: as a sign of respect the seller will fry the *panelle* only to order, with the result that the fritter can get nowhere near one's lips for a good 15 minutes. When and if this happens to you, you must rejoice in this suffering, and bear in mind that the alternative is a roll assembled with ready-made fritters that have congealed – these normally serve only for display purposes. Such treatment is considered a slight and is reserved for uninstructed tourists and for pariahs.

Other specialities to be found in the *rosticceria* include *cazzille* (potato croquettes), *quaglie* (slices of fried aubergine, broccoli and artichoke in batter), grilled song-bird and mandarin oranges, which in the city are referred to in the feminine, *arancine* – the masculine form, *arancini*, being considered provincial and there-fore beneath notice. To taste the best *arancine* you have to leave the city centre and go to a bar that was provisionally closed some years ago on the grounds of deficient hygiene. A small scandal ensued wherein the locals (aside from jealous competitors) lined up unflinchingly behind the storekeeper. The prevailing thesis was that if the kitchen really was filthy that only meant that the *grascia*, the muck, was an integral part of the *arancine*. Whoever decides to eat one does so in full knowledge. At worst, one might do as with a cigarette, and write on the paper tissue, or on the item itself, 'This product is dangerous to your health'.

To this same family of soft-core edibles – but soft-core only by comparison with such hard-core items as *stig-ghiòla* and the like – belong two subdivisions: the *sfin-cione*, a kind of pizza with onions, mare's milk cheese and anchovies, which are sold in bakeries and off barrows, and for which the same rules of hygiene apply as for the *arancine*; and then seafood such as sea-urchins and squid, frugally eaten at seafood counters which, in recent years, have tended to expand to the point of becoming proper trattorias. Beware of the squid, served on large plates, sliced up in front of the customer and dressed only with lemon: it is hard as nails and tough as old boots. That's how the city-dwellers like it, because any tenderness is considered effeminate. A person has to suffer, even when attending to the pleasures of the table.

Leaving aside the ostentatious machismo of gastron-omy, there is one foodstuff which above all others in the city is always of paramount excellence. And it is the polar opposite of the baroque delicacies described above: bread. This will have something to do with the water, the salt or what have you. Maybe something to do with the *grascia* mentioned above.

The fact remains that the bread in the city is the best to be found anywhere. If you still don't feel up to leaving your room, have them send up a bread roll. Only one. Ask if they might possibly send up one reground, with a scat-tering of sesame seeds. They'll ask you, 'Is that all?'

Your answer will be 'No.' Spoil yourself and trust them. Tell them it is just a fancy you cannot resist. Just one roll will do. At all events, bread in the city is poor man's bread, conceived to be eaten without any trimmings. No need for any. Which is why when you are in a restaurant waiting to be served it is hard to resist the temptation to stuff yourself with bread.

It only remains to speak of the desserts, something for which the city is famous. The cassata is a symbol of this reputation. But in its triumph of triglycerides and colours baroquely assembled, the cassata merely represents that which the city-dwellers wish to display of themselves. The equivalent to the traditional cart, a mass of ornaments and plumes. In contrast with the joyous extroversion of the classic cassata, maybe the almost black-and-white sobriety of the cassata *al forno* needs to be considered: here the outside envelope of tender pastry is content to screen the treasure of ricotta within. The fact is, if it is possible to trace one characteristic the city-dwellers all have in common, it must definitely be found in the introversion of the cassata *al forno*, more than in the extroversion of the traditional cassata, a dessert that is all façade. As a general rule, the cassata is an old-fashioned sweet that is only bought as a present, to discharge an obligation, to make a payment in kind for some professional service. The same holds true for the *buccellato*, a repulsive variant on the strudel: it is given as a present at Christmas, a tiny bit of it is eaten, and the rest goes into the dustbin before Epiphany. This is because pastries on the island, almost all of which are of Arab inspiration, are very high in calories. They might well represent a nutritional experiment for astronauts, the way they address the need to contain the maximum nutritive value in the minimum bulk. A slice of cassata is the equivalent of a full meal. The same is true of *cannoli* (cream horns) and other local specialities – line them all up and they make a whole nursery rhyme of assorted sugars adapted to the various times of year and the requirements of the calendar: melon ice, blancmange, *martorana* fruit, lamb-shaped meringues, *kubbaita*, honeycake, candied chestnuts, *puma 'ncilippati*, sugar babies, *mustazzola, cuccìa* (made with wheat flour, milk, sugar and cinnamon), *minne di vergine*, '*patate*', *sfinci di San Giuseppe*, keys of St Peter, Sacred Hearts, Turks' heads, *sammartinelli, reginelle* and lastly the latest fantastic invention from a pastry cook in Via Colonna Rotta: the *torta Setteveli*, a chocolate confection destined to outlast the vagaries of time and taste.

The requirement for lightness envisaged by modern life leaves us to predict the extinction, or the preservation in a museum, of many of these sweet specialities. This fate has recently overtaken the 'Triumph of Greed', a high calorie bombe of green pistachio, compared with which the cassata is dieters' food. The last people to make it were the nuns in the Convent of the Virgins, at the back of the Teatro Biondo, and then only to order. A city legend claims that the milk used for the ricotta was produced by the nuns personally. Today the weight and elaboration of the 'Triumph of Greed' is still remembered, but even this memory will have been lost in a few years' time.

In the panorama of desserts, the ice cream deserves its own particular niche. Among the cafés that double as ice cream parlours with tables outside in the summer, it is good to go to a certain café in the Foro Italico, where some rare specialities are still available, like rice and Chantilly or *scorsonera* and cinnamon, unknown elsewhere. This café is one of the inexplicably fascinating ones in a city that is, taken as a whole, inexplicably fascinating. It is good to go there, but nobody knows why: the sea should be just across the way, but the view is blocked, the waiters are casual, and the condition of the furnishings is such that an expert could deduce from them how far along the summer has got: from 14 July, the Feast of St Rosalia, the tablecloths smell, and the suspicion arises that they only get laundered in September. It is one of those ancient establishments where a fly in your *granita* contributes to the charm of the place. You can always discard the fly, the charm subsists.

Compared to classic pastries, ice cream would in theory be considered a lighter dessert. But the ice cream is straightaway accompanied by a brioche: the brioche with ice cream is one of the major contributions the city has made to civilization – very well, but kiss goodbye to lightness. So here too a mystery remains: how come that in a more or less African latitude, a pastry, and more generally a cuisine, that is so baroque in its heaviness has found favour? The only plausible explanation is that we are looking at a variant of the *cupio dissolvi*. Death wish. Perhaps it is in the pages of *The Leopard* that the key to this sentiment is to be found. The Prince explains to Chevalley: 'All self-expression [of the islanders], even the most violent, is really wish-fulfilment; our sensuality is a hankering for oblivion, our shooting and knifing a hankering for death; our languor, our exotic ices, a hankering for voluptuous immobility, that is, for death again.'*

*Translation by Archibald Colquhoun, from *The Leopard* (Collins Harvill: 1960).

7

The sea does not bathe the city

It could be that one of the reasons why you are hesitating to leave your hotel is the news you have gleaned from the papers on the low standard of living hereabouts. There's not much to be said on that score. Numbers are numbers. For the city-dwellers one of the worst moments of the year comes when *Sole 24 Ore* publishes a list of Italian cities in order of living standards. There's a moment of general anxiety because there are changes in the town halls, and in this listing the city always hovers around the hundred mark. Sometimes it climbs to 99, sometimes it drops to 101, but that's where she's fixed. Some years it looks as if there's been a slight improvement, at least in certain areas. Expectations rise. But every time the bludgeon falls: 100. 99. 101.

With the publication of the table there always follows a week of discussions among the city-dwellers, private comments and public declarations. The town hall questions the yardsticks, it clutches at sporadic factors going against the stream, it heaps all the blame on the previous administration. But it is now 20 years since they started compiling this table, and the city never budges from her spot at number 100, or only imperceptibly, and never decisively upwards, not even when at a certain point she seemed to have become the Italian capital of the new Renaissance.

Usually the mayor observes that if anyone should be concerned about it, it should be the Provincial Governor, given that the tabulation is based on the entire province. Here, though, the responsibilities become more fluid and sink into the sand. Then the daily papers always contrive to dig up a poet, or an artist, or television comedian ready to insist that he wouldn't live in Bolzano (the town that always tops the chart) for love nor money – it's way too cold. The city-dwellers read this and smirk: even this annual humiliation is absorbed and converted into a shamefaced pride. To hell with *Sole 24 Ore* and its tabulation. What are these Milanese on about? What do they know about life, living in their eternal fog, and if anyone takes ill in the street no one will stop to lend a hand.

Whether or not anyone would stop in Milan to give you a hand if you were taken ill in the street, while in the city everyone stops to help, is still a moot point. However, the meteorological component is not in fact included among the yardsticks adopted in compiling the table. And this is comforting. It may be a commonplace, but the fact of being able to count on a prevalence of sunny days helps defeat the depression of living in the Italian city that is 100 down the list. Even on grey days everyone is possessed of the expectation of things improving, which keeps the heart open to hope. This morning it's raining, later perhaps it won't be, tomorrow maybe it will be raining, but not for the whole day – and this is always better than a winter of lowering skies, day after day, with no hope of change. Commonplaces may well be banal, but sometimes none the less true for this. *Sole 24 Ore* ought to bear this in mind.

The argument does, nonetheless, come perilously close to being groundless. For at least 200 years all Europe's physicians advised their patients to make a trip to the island to cure any respiratory diseases. The cure was often worse than the disease. Wagner himself, who came here for the winter, saw his favourite son, Siegfried, fall sick with a pernicious fever, and at that point ceased to believe in the virtues of the salubrious climate he had come in search of. And so it goes: the number of wealthy visitors who have come to the island for health reasons is beyond counting; they would arrive in the city and here they would receive the *coup de grâce* in those poorly heated houses which they were not used to. Should you pluck up the courage, my dear visitor, go and pay a visit to the cemetery of Santa Maria di Gesù, where the number of gravestones with foreign names is also beyond counting. Try to imagine the fate of such indigent rich folk who arrived here to die far from home, with their lungs blocked and their hearts open to hope.

In these parts the clichés relating to the climate often take the form of a song: 'Enough that there's the sun, enough that there's the sea ...' More than enough. But having reached this point, we have to channel the stereotypes. The sun – OK. But the sea? Who in the city has ever set eyes on the sea?

If you were a more enterprising visitor you should try the whole of the coastline, from south-east to north-west, from Settecannoli to Sferracavallo, if you can. See if you can keep your car as close to the sea as possible, stopping each time you catch a glimpse of it, or it seems within reach. From the moment you set out, all you'll see is an endless succession of walls and billboards. At Acqua dei Corsari the sea will at last come into view; but it would be as well were it invisible, fetid as it is, and fetid as the beach is.

Then comes La Bandita, where the sea appears every now and then like a washboard of brown scum with a rim of sand and detritus, more detritus than sand. For at least the last 50 years this stretch of sea has been dying. There's supposed to be a recovery plan for the coast, but as it is much the same since the 1980s, you don't hold out much hope.

At Romagnolo there are signs forbidding sea-bathing, but they are redundant because the brown scum is enough on its own to discourage the bather. There are one or two old houses by the shore but nothing newly built. Not even the most shameless jerry-builder would dream of putting anything up on the shore of a sea such as this.

At Sant' Erasmo we come to the start of a line of walls and gateways behind which there are no houses, but scrap-iron dumps, small businesses that have found it convenient to sit on the seashore. Evidently it costs less. At Sant' Erasmo there is also the estuary of the Oreto, a river worthy of this sea. Beyond that you get the Istituto Padre Messina, which marks the beginning of the Foro Italico, a.k.a. La Marina, which used to be the city's seafront, except that the sea is now 200 metres further out. The rubble from the air raids has been discharged here, and the sea has withdrawn as a result. Up until a few years ago, on this tongue of land they had sited a public recreation ground in a provisionally definitive manner, as also a small piazza in white marble with a team of statues of saints brought in to perform a miracle and upgrade the locality. The miracle never worked, and sanctity was relocated to the Zen quarter, to attempt what was maybe an even more complicated miracle.

And, on this terrain, the gardeners paid by the Commune and those employed by a private firm have been quarrelling over the best way to make a lawn in the English manner, without every reaching a solution that could cope with the salt content for more than six months. Now there's the odd tree, and if you really concentrate you may spot, right at the back, a line of what looks like blue.

Then there's La Cala. La Cala is the old port, which now plays host to the pleasure-sailing fraternity and to an environmental disaster, half and half. About the seawater in La Cala, which assumes a colour tending towards a washed-out white and a consistency that is oily, legends flourish. They say that the anglers' hooks have for years been pulling in only mice. Every ship owner in the world finds here a perfect cemetery in which to scuttle vessels which would be too expensive to bury at sea. They say that with the arrival of each new vessel to be stripped at La Cala, a swarm of human ants arrive to set about the stripping. They carry off everything that is moveable, then sink the carcass. Now and then the relic fails to submerge, making navigation problematic; sometimes it is the mainmast that protrudes, and this becomes in its turn the hitching post for other vessels being decommissioned, in the expectation that they too will come to their moment of disappearance.

Continuing on beyond La Cala we come to a row of palaces. When you get there don't forget to take a good look at the balconies of the main façades of these buildings: they face inland. Having to choose between a view of the sea and a view of other palaces, the architects who built them freely opted for the latter solution. Leonardo Sciascia has already noted that the city turns her back on the sea. The city-dwellers are happy enough to resist the temptation of a sea-blue panorama. You can smell the sea, you can assume it's there, but there's scarcely a spot where you can set eyes on it, nor does anyone wish to do so. Even when a provisional plan was made for the Foro Italico, people straightaway started using the marble seating the wrong way, so as to face not the sea, as they had been expected to do, but the city, which has always been on view to everybody.

Further on there is the harbour area, on which it would be unfair to express an opinion: in every big city the harbour is inexplicably the last place that offers a view of the sea. You have to keep to the right, trusting that if there's a Customs House, there must be a harbour, and the harbour must be on the sea it stands to reason. And yet the sea disappears for several kilometres. You enter Viale Cristoforo Colombo, and at once you're among shipyards, which is encouraging. Not only do they represent the city's prime industry – at number two, would you believe, is the Teatro Massimo – but they must, of their nature, lie on the seashore. The sea really is there, it's a question of making sure. You have to believe in it, and press on: Arenella, Acquasanta, Vergine Maria.

A little tourist harbour comes into view, but there's no way of getting close to it unless you have one of the motor launches moored to the pier. The sea is only just beyond, and, as always happens, suggests profound reflections, especially when it takes the shape of a bay. Were you to find yourself here, you would, like every good tourist, be inclined to stop and reflect. One of the most noble thoughts that would come to mind when faced with the majestic spectacle spread out before you would be: how on earth do all these people have so much money that they can own all these boats? Isn't the city's gross domestic product on the low side? Isn't the enterprise culture here a wan chimera? And, if they are not business tycoons, who are these folk who can afford a yacht?

Come to that, you'll be mulling over such questions the whole time as you stand in front of those concealed gateways beyond which you might catch a glimpse of small villas masquerading as castles built on the cliff edge. Or before the profusion of luxury boutiques along Via Libertà. If Vuitton decides to open a branch right here, it means he will have worked out the potential client profile in advance. If at the pan-European convention of Volvo and BMW agents, the dealers from the city are welcomed with open arms, there has to be a reason.

The only thing is that, compared with elsewhere, the people in the money are in no hurry to make a public display of it. Ostentation stops at the bare minimum, and in private. In the circle of the owner's friends, the yacht is of course a luxury to be enjoyed to the full. But the really rich take great care, if they are throwing a party, to ensure that no photo appears in the papers. What they strive for is the appearance of a *demi-mondain*. It is the *demi-mondain* who will wear a dark suit and is vain enough to let himself be spotted as he climbs the steps of the Teatro Massimo, to undergo the social tedium of an operatic soirée. The truly rich keep away from the place, just as they want to avoid featuring on a list of big contributors. Why otherwise is it so difficult in the city to find any kind of sponsor? Why is it that the local football team has always had such a battle to acquire a president, some native businessman ready to show his face as well as his money? A couple of club presidents have met a sorry end owing to the over-exposure to which they submitted. For the really big operators in the city, to live a secret life is the cardinal rule. And this is not only out of the wish to avoid attracting the attention of the tax authorities.

But the boats have to be kept somewhere, and anyway these considerations are not for the moment germane. We have to keep going, we are still looking out for the sea. We have to manage to touch it, though it won't be easy. The spectacular hotel that lies along the way is called Villa Igeia. If you were staying here, you could see the sea merely by stepping out onto your balcony. But you couldn't step into the sea: bathing prohibited.

So we must proceed onwards, hugging the shore as far as possible. The sea comes into view 1 kilometre further on, at L'Arenella, then disappears and reappears, a succession of picture postcard scenes, fleeting but unforgettable. All the way to L'Addaura we have one gated wall after another, the gates chained up so as to obstruct the view of the sea, one imagines, for those not entitled to it. What about you, visitor, what rights can you claim? You, who come perhaps from a city with no sea to it, how come it's right here that you want to greet it?

Onwards. The samples of seascape that occasionally offer themselves to our eyes don't add up to much, and our jaunt has now turned into a 20-kilometre trek, with not many kilometres left to reach what will have been our goal from the start: Mondello – the seaside town most favoured by the city-dwellers. The last ramparts of Monte Pellegrino must first be circumvented; here's a last curve to travel past, a last blind railing to ignore, and here we are in Mondello, looking like a picture postcard of itself. Try to imagine it.

Try to imagine the bay as it would have appeared to the Milanese engineer Pietro Scaglia, who climbed Monte Pellegrino one day in 1902, looked down, and seeing what was in those days a seaside marsh, had an inkling of what Mondello might become. Possibly he imagined it with fewer billboards and fewer villas than we have there today, but the framework and everything is just the same. So he left Milan and settled on the island to pursue his intuition. He drew up a recovery plan and parcelled out the land in the whole bay area, then sat back and waited.

While engineer Scaglia was waiting, a competitor, the Società Italo-Belga, put in a land use application similar to his, practically identical. Eventually it was the second application that won, the Società Italo-Belga's, and engineer Pietro Scaglia, who had sunk his entire fortune and his own life into the project, committed suicide in despair. Somewhere in Mondello there is a little alley-way bearing his name.

Land reclamation and attribution is what happened next, and how! Time was when there was a golf course and a tram connecting Mondello with the city – it ran through the Parco della Favorita. The houses were built to look like those in Ostend, because in their haste to parcel up the land they had decided to copy a Belgian model. Hence the elegant yet incongruous air of some of the villas to be found in the residential area.

The original nucleus was a cluster of fishermen's cottages gathered round the tunny fishery. All that's left now of the tunny fishery is the tower in the piazza, hemmed in by bars and little restaurants which are active mostly on Saturdays and Sundays during July and August, when the city-dwellers go pouring out to Mondello, turning it into a gastronomic village where you eat badly and expensively. True that in a town of this sort, where hanging out in the open air is an advantage to be exploited 300 days a year, virtually the only cafés that get the sun and have a view of the sea are to be found here, on the piazza.

The rapport that the city-dwellers maintain with Mondello is novel one. You have the paradoxical situation of rural retreats being built just 5 or 6 kilometres from the city apartment blocks. Even so each year, in June, families solemnly move house and fetch up here for three months, where they have the consolation of a seaside holiday. Once again what is evident is the tendency of the city-dwellers to squander their assets. They take only the worst of Mondello, the high season overcrowding, and discard the best: autumn, winter, spring, when the chaos is elsewhere, the cold is simply cool, the heat pleasantly warm.

Above all, between June and September, what's become of the sea? During those months the beach is cut off by the bathing cabins, which here are tribally known as *huts*. The city-dwellers maintain their own kind of rapport even with their huts. In particular, those who cannot afford a country house tend to consider their bathing hut as if it were one, and cram it with all manner of creature comforts. Using the hut as their pied-à-terre, the families turn up early in the morning and only resign themselves to returning to town in the late evening. You should try coming here in July. The open areas between the huts are known as courtyards, quite properly, because they reproduce exactly the habitat of the old-style southern courtyard and the social life that went on there. Until the sun goes down – and beyond, by the light of acetylene lamps – people play cards in these beach courtyards, eat *pasta al forno*, and chat. All this until at least midnight; then everything is stowed away inside the hut – tables, chairs, lamps, furniture and knick-knacks – and back they go to town. They are aware, however, that this is only for the few hours devoted inevitably to sleep; tomorrow they'll be back.

In the winter Mondello is different. Then, because you can see the sea from here, you can also touch it. Moreover, you can touch it without reference to any beach hut. At a certain point they even decided to remove (but only in the depth of winter) the green gate closing off the approach to the beach, that obstructed the view of the bay. Formally, its task was to prevent 'an improper enjoyment of the beach', whatever that is supposed to mean. The beach is made for walking on, and anyway the gateway is riddled with gaps. What then? The only plausible reason for keeping it there is to stop anyone looking at the seascape. Even so, each spring it is put back in place, and again it's so long to the sea view.

This gateway in Mondello is one of the best symbols of the rapport that exists between the city and the sea. A rapport that may be summed up as: the city-dwellers don't give a damn for the sea. In the conviction that they belong to a race of gods, they turn their backs on the sea with the same arrogance with which a rich man would use a bank-note to light his cigar. Except that the city-dwellers are not plutocrats. Indeed, they dress in rags, however you look at them, but that does not stop them from flaunting their big ideas, ill-founded though they are. The sea is theirs, but they have decided to do without it. They shrug it off like a tip left in a restaurant as they're called away on more urgent business, more important considerations. What this more urgent business, these more important considerations are exactly, no one has ever discovered.

But the truth is they don't give a damn about the sea. You only have to watch their reactions on discovering, as happens every now and then, that even at Mondello the sea is a seething mass of streptococci and staphylococci. The town hall orders a ban on sea-bathing, and what happens with the folk in the bathing huts? Nothing. The waterside card games continue, the pans of *pasta al forno* continue to be passed around beneath the beach umbrellas, and sea-bathing is replaced by showers. Only a fraction of the population objects. In most cases there is a clear preference for showing that one is above this kind of setback. To pay for a beach-cabin by the sea when at a certain point the sea is off-limits, this is considered normal. Complain? Oh, they'll complain all right! But to protest would be out of place; perhaps even a touch vulgar. The city can drive one to despair on occasions, but she is never desperate herself. She breeds despair without herself despairing.

Behind Monte Gallo, continuing along the coast, there should be Fossa del Gallo, which is almost free from contamination. But if you want to pass through this place, which features on the map as a nature reserve, you have to pay a toll to a private party. The road along the shore is his, never mind the nature reserve. Beyond Monte Gallo comes Sferracavallo, another seaside town, but by this point you would be entitled to feel tired and demoralized, after discovering that around about the city, despite every reassurance the map may furnish, there is no sea, or if there is, it is invisible, or filthy, or in private ownership.

I can understand you. One could very nearly feel that you were quite right in not wanting to leave your hotel. But this is not so. For reasons hard to explain, this is not so.

8

The villas, the gardens

The same attitude of unwarranted hauteur with which the city-dwellers regard the sea is also directed towards any public green space. The houses may have little gardens, that's something to which all aspire, and that's one thing; so is a terrace with pretty flowers. But the city's public gardens are considered *res nullius* and are as such treated with total disdain. The benches are torn out and carried off for private use. And if they are made of marble, they get splintered now and then to ensure that no one gets the idea of sitting on them to contemplate the greenery, such as it is. The paths in the English Garden and in many other public gardens are asphalted to avoid the risk of turning one's ankles. The flower-beds are far from copious. In general, the enjoyment of green space is considered a romantic extravagance, an impulse to be kept under control. The important, more urgent things are not to be found here.

Some years ago there were swans on a small pond in Villa Giulia. One day they vanished. An enquiry was held to establish where the two birds had ended up, but the result was inconclusive. Then a second pair was provided, and three days later these too had vanished. And again, and yet again. It became a kind of urban crime serial: Who was making off with the Villa Giulia swans? The keepers at the Villa, after the fourth incident, organized night patrols to keep an eye on the pond to see who and what was behind this traffic in stolen swans, and heaven knows where they were sold. They remained in ambush until they managed to lay hands on the culprits. These turned out to be members of an extended family of local paupers, whose defence was that they had not stolen the swans to sell them but to eat them. And this is a good example of the private enterprise exploitation to which, for reasons of *force majeure*, the public authorities have to submit.

In the repertory of the city's green spaces we find the Parco d'Orleans, whose opening hours are subject to variation. There's no knowing whether you will have the luck to find it open when you turn up. It is a pretty garden, well maintained, with aviaries full of all manner of birds.

There are the Botanical Gardens, which the city-dwellers always maintain are the largest in Europe – maybe they're right. What is certain is that to get in you have to pay a tiny entrance fee, with the result that, apart from the odd student, you'll never meet a soul along the pathways. Just the place for solitary meditation.

There's the park of Villa Malfitano, the seat of a foundation that keeps the place going by opening it at infrequent intervals.

There's the mastodontic rarity of the great *ficus* in Villa Garibaldi, in Piazza Marina, which the city-dwellers always maintain is the largest in Europe. What is certain is that in the Botanical Gardens of the same city there is a bigger one.

But if we're looking for sheer size, there's above all the Parco della Favorita. This was a Bourbon hunting estate. When the royal family came to the island – whether under the constraint of Napoleon's invasion or of popular uprisings in Naples – they would sometimes take refuge in the miniature Chinese palace, an elaborate building in perpetual process of restoration, on the edge of the park.

Not many cities can boast a green space like the Favorita, stuck in the very middle of the residential zone. Thanks to its acreage this is a park that allows the city to breathe, and it is a safety factor in the statistics of per capita green space. Such is the Favorita: it helps the city-dwellers to breathe, but is virtually invisible, because they take little account of their park. They go by and forget all about it. So blasé are they about it that someone has, on the strength of this indifference, contrived over the years to fence off and annex stretches of the public green space, installing a series of private kitchen gardens. Every ten years the interlopers are denounced, but the kitchen gardens carry on there because the city-dwellers as a rule only remember the Favorita on Easter Mondays, when they repair thither in a simulation of a day in the country. On these occasions they bring with them a good deal more than a picnic – picnic's not in it! Along the path-ways in the park they carry their entire kitchens, their dining rooms and bedrooms. Ideally they install their toilet behind a bush, after which they settle in and stay there till nightfall.

Even on Sundays, when their leisure time leaves them sufficient margin for the contemplation of nature, the

Favorita is spurned more than it is favoured. The road out to Mondello crosses this green phenomenon, but not even on holidays is a stop in the park advisable. Not to speak of the other six days of the week, when the Favorita is a tract of land fought over between motor traffic and the human fauna comprising joggers and prostitutes, with certain intermediate species hard to classify. A well-ensconced population which makes the Favorita redolent of a fairy tale forest crawling with fairy-trollops and ghouls to scare young and old alike.

Some years ago a gentleman went there to die. They found him chained to a tree; and another gentleman who happened to be passing made off with his wallet. They arrested him on a charge of homicide, but he was able to prove that the charge should be reduced to one of larceny. Having discovered the body, he supposed he was entitled to a small reward. In such a context anyone who stops is suspect, and then he's done for. Which is why the motorists dash through the Favorita without ever stopping.

One other thing the city-dwellers do about the Favorita is leave their dogs there. This may happen because the municipal dog-pound is in the park, and they hope that their puppy will be adopted. Or else it's only because they imagine that a pretty park so full of greenery must be a fine place in which to be abandoned, given that at worst there will always be something there for them to eat. The result of this is that in addition to the already disturbing population of the Favorita, we have periodically to add packs of dogs wild with hunger. With time these dogs become ever more truculent, and it has happened that they have pursued and bitten a pedestrian. If you don't take care, if you don't do something about it, little by little the dogs tend to become the true owners of the pathways through the park. And as we have this recurrent theory that things happen in the city sooner and in a somewhat more bloodthirsty manner than elsewhere, the possibility today exists of having to confront a canine uprising. Perhaps, the doomsayers may come to think, a great worldwide revolution is starting right here. Perhaps, after a period of human domination, it is the dogs who are destined to become the master race on Earth. Perhaps soon dogs will take the place of humans, just as humans at a given time displaced the dinosaurs. Man may indeed survive for a time, but his civilization is destined to become obsolete. Of course, this thesis is at present only guesswork, and you must take no account of it to feed the fears that at this moment are inhibiting you. This is not to be thought of. And yet, there is no knowing how it will all end, because history is still unfolding and there are dogs all over the place and they do tend to take over the green spaces, confident in the notion that they are nobody's property.

What is a no man's land, a vast mass and yet itself invisible and thus the umpteenth proof of the city-dwellers' collective myopia, is the mountain that looms up plumb in the middle of the city. You cannot fail to see it, and yet it remains invisible. Or, if it is seen, no account is taken of it, not least because the two access roads are periodically closed to traffic owing to rock falls. Monte Pellegrino is the most eye-catching relief feature in the Conca d'Oro.

The city-dwellers, however, manage to celebrate its profile by always quoting the same words of Goethe who, arriving by sea, defined it as 'the most beautiful promontory in the world'. Two hundred years later, when a surge of pride takes hold of the poetic soul of us dwellers on its flanks, the best we can come up with is 'the most beautiful promontory in the world'.

On the summit of Monte Pellegrino there is the sanctuary of the city's patron saint, Rosalia Sinibaldi, in whose honour a single day is deemed insufficient: 4 September, her feast day, is the day for a pilgrimage to her shrine, while in July we have five days of festivities – the so-called Festino. When the Viceroy Caracciolo made a bid, in his rash attempt at enlightenment, to reduce expenditure by cutting out two of the festival's five days, a second Sicilian Vespers was on the point of erupting – and once again for futile reasons.

According to tradition, the festival ends with a solemn procession and fireworks. Many tourists come from all over the world especially to attend it, even while there exists a small number of residents who, conversely, programme their holidays so as to be sure to be well out of the way on those days. Notwithstanding other methods of political evaluation, the local authority stakes its entire future on that night: should public opinion be disappointed by the fireworks, the mayor's fate is sealed.

Rosalia Sinibaldi earned the charge of patroness of the city when she undermined a quartet of other saints – Agatha, Christina, Ninfa and Oliva – who even in collaboration were unable to see off a fierce pestilence. All that was needed was to go to Monte Pellegrino and fetch the relics of the new saint, carry them in procession, and the city was saved. In recent years Rosalia has acquired a sort of auxiliary in the shape of St Benedict the Moor, who could well represent the multicultural soul of the city. But never mind the intentions of those who govern us, St Benedict the Moor has not yet been able to enter into the hearts of the devout, and certainly not to the point of competing with St Rosalia. First let there be a plague, and let him stop it, and then we'll have another think.

The grotto of St Rosalia is on the summit of Monte Pellegrino, set within a sanctuary, all lit up with votive candles, very affecting. There's this casket containing the statue of the saint. Rosalia is in a semi-reclining position, one hand and elbow supporting her head. On the ground beside her are a large scattering of coins and banknotes. Indeed a whole mass of them, so as to hide the floor beneath. There are also lighters, rings, gold watches left by those in the throes of veneration. On the walls of the grotto hang the ex-votos: noses, breasts, feet, all in silver, whichever part of the body has been miraculously cured.

So mystical is the atmosphere that no sooner have the eyes grown accustomed to the semi-darkness, they cannot but be raised heavenwards, where the upper reaches of the grotto are almost entirely covered in a network of guttering large and small, made of aluminium, though it too looks like silver. It serves to reroute the drips resulting from humidity away from visitors' heads, where they may do less damage. However the water is considered miraculous and so is collected and made the object of devout recycling.

Monte Pellegrino and the Parco della Favorita are two of those places that the city neither knows nor cares how to exploit. Then there are those places that the city seems to be on the point of exploiting, or seems to have exploited up to a point, but then decides to exploit no longer. One of these is Villa Trabia, to mention another potential park in the heart of the city which simultaneously exists and does not exist; so much in evidence as to remain invisible. A park which carries the weight of a history that is in its own way significant.

They say that Villa Trabia was rescued from parcelling up into plots by a subtle ploy. It came one day to the notice of the prince who lived there that the park was to be sacrificed to satisfy one of the periodic expansions of the city's building programme. According to the new urban plan, an extension of Via Santorre di Santarosa was to pass slap through the park, which was enough to evoke the horrible word 'expropriation'. So the prince chose the exact point where the new road was to pass and placed there a marble column and, atop the column, a small statue. Then he called on a friend of his in the department responsible for monuments, and within a week the statue had a protection order placed on it as an artistic treasure of inestimable value. This is how it came about that the street stopped short of the park and the villa was saved.

This is probably one of the city's myths, but it could perfectly well be true. At all events, like other similar stories relating to Villa Trabia, there is some truth in its components. One item of truth is of course the villa itself: the *casena* built in the eighteenth century, and the park of more than 53,000 square metres, with statues and fountains by Ignazio Marabitti – the whole thing miraculously slotted into the jerry-building boom of the 1950s and 1960s. There really was a statue, which got stolen in the 1980s, its supporting column being knocked down. Now only the pedestal survives. Statue or not, they built the road a little further out, in the 1970s. It is now called Via Piersanti Mattarella and it splits the park in two, leaving only the umbilical cord of a stone bridge.

No one even knows who the mythical prince was who proved so averse to the speculators. For the last two members of the dynasty, Raimondo and Galvano, neither the chronology nor the aims coincide, seeing that at a certain point they would have cheerfully sold off some bits of the park to shore up their financial shipwreck. They could not – so much the better.

Don Raimondo and Don Galvano Lanza di Trabia were not, actually, princes. Their parents were Giuseppe, Prince of Trabia, and an already-married woman. Little Galvano and Raimondo were brought up by a grandmother who one day, unable to endure the thought of the little ones growing up without any titles of nobility, went and knelt at the feet of Mussolini asking him to intercede in a matter of heraldry. So Mussolini persuaded the king to promulgate a law effective for only 24 hours. A window of opportunity opened up and immediately closed off, with only the heir of Count Volpi and the two Lanza boys being able to avail themselves of it. Thenceforth they did not become exactly 'Lanza princes of Trabia' but 'Princes Lanza of Trabia', pray note the difference. It seems negligible and yet it is everything, if we credit certain details.

So the two little princes grew up and shone, and kept going both within and outside of the aristocratic ambience that survived the last war. Raimondo once fetched up on the cover of *Domenica del Corriere* thanks to a duel he fought right in the heart of the city, when duels were an extravagance of the past. Then he went to Spain on a spy mission for Galeazzo Ciano – unless he went on a mission for the Americans. At all events, off he went to see what was happening in Spain, where he fought on one of the opposing sides and ended up with a medal. What is certain is that when the Allies arrived in the city, Charles Poletti installed his headquarters right there in Villa Trabia. It would seem that Prince Raimondo was anxious to have him as guest before the visitor could declare himself an occupier.

Every source agrees in ascribing to the two last princes a natural predisposition towards merrymaking, an ideal to which they devoted their entire lives. Raimondo, the more braggart of the pair, not only piloted aeroplanes, he drove racing cars, gambled at cards, and rejoiced in scandalizing the more staid members of his class, larding his conversation with swear words. At one point it was his pleasure to become president of the city's football club. They say that he ran the football transfers while in the bath, where emissaries from other clubs found him immersed.

But most of all, Raimondo loved women. They say that among his lovers were Rita Hayworth and Evita Peron.

He married the actress Olga Villi, who, it was said, stood on the finest pair of legs in Italy. With her he produced two girls, and it seems that one day, while he was on his travels, he sent her a four-word telegram: 'Finally Possess Splendid Squaw.'

Galvano too laboured in the vineyards of love, only for matrimony to arrive, so we are told, but a short while before he died. If it actually took place, it was a secret wedding and lasted only a few days because a league of friends persuaded him to back-track. The lady, who had already left two husbands bobbing in her wake, was satisfied with an honourable settlement and that's where the matter ended.

Guests at Villa Trabia, in times to which the memory still reaches back, included Tazio Nuvolari, Joan Fontaine, Clark Gable, Edda Ciano, Aristotle Onassis, and Queen Elena. Among those who slept at the villa we must add Errol Flynn, who crossed the ocean to take part at the Arenella in a cloak-and-dagger movie, *The Gentleman Pirate*. And this, mythical though it may seem, appears to be the plain truth: Errol Flynn at the Arenella.

Then there is the story of when, after the war, a certain Prince of Paternò, being a resident in the villa, jumped from the first floor balcony thanks to some ghosts he claimed to have seen in his bedroom. In the collective opinion of the domestic staff he was not merely a drunkard but a fraidy-cat. Anyway, he did himself no damage with his jump.

Don Raimondo Lanza di Trabia also jumped one day from a balcony, only he died. His balcony was on an upper floor of the Eden Hotel in Rome. He jumped just as he found himself, stark naked. Legend states that he had only recently discovered that the high life he had been leading up to that point was now beyond his grasp. They say that the discovery that he had become a pauper drove him to visit an artisan to recover certain items of porcelain he had taken in for repair. When it came to the time to pay, the artisan refused to defer any further the settlement of a large sum which Don Raimondo now owed him. The prince departed in silence, leaving the porcelain as a pledge, along with all the pride he had been able to muster. The estate had long since ceased to be lucrative, as had also the big tunny-works at Trabia and the sulphur mines at Pasquasìa. Or at any rate they had ceased to be lucrative for the family, given that the estate and the sulphur mines continued to be productive, but to someone else's benefit. After the death of Don Raimondo, Domenico Modugno wrote a song in his memory, which has become famous: '*L'Uomo in frac*', 'The Man in the Tailcoat'.

That left Don Galvano now a pauper. But it was a splendid poverty, nurtured by virtue of the remaining impetus of his erstwhile squandered life. During the years he survived, spent mostly in Rome, whenever he returned he would be given free accommodation in the aristocrats' club, the Circolo dell' Unione, which was renting the *casena* in Villa Trabia and its immediate outbuildings, from a bank, which had become owner thanks to an uncleared debt. When he died he owed money to the petrol station and the tobacconist, debts recently contracted; even in the summer he would leave the house rubbing his hands for cold, cold that only he felt. To compensate for this, many people among the rich and famous came to his funeral. The waiters recollect seeing a car window lowered and a hand reaching out with a 50,000-lire tip – this from the attorney Agnelli.

In recent times Villa Trabia has been the object of litigation over a number of years. The property was bought by the local government which fought to evict the club until further resistance by the tenants would have been out of keeping with aristocratic good form. The Public Office of Culture was installed in the *casena* – this is when policies regarding the city's culture were set in train. The villa has hosted spectacular exhibitions and events. The park may be visited freely, barring certain restrictive bylaws, which even regulate the use of children's tricycles.

Today the park maintains 134 of the 2,796 botanical species listed at the end of the nineteenth century in the catalogue of the Terre Rosse, as the grounds were known. The variety of orchids grown in the prince's hothouses numbered 286, and 30 the number of gardeners employed around the estate to keep it as a kind of second Botanical Gardens, with gazelles and guinea fowl scratching about in their enclosure, and five colossal *ficus* to look picturesque.

But this story or fable does, all things considered, have a happy ending: the princes die, true enough, but the villa is rescued and families, however middle class, can now go in there for a stroll.

Is this tale enough, with its happy ending, to overcome the fears you suffer as a traveller confined to your room? Take care: time flies. Force yourself to believe that out there we have a city full of surprises, even pleasant ones, rich in anecdotes that taken together form a considerable history.

9

The practice of auto-exoticism

When the city-dwellers speak of their past they tend to indulge in a measure of waffle. To show off a bit. Here too, as in Naples and maybe in every town of southern Italy, the story is told of the cab-driver arguing with a fare from the north. Let us called the man a Milanese for the sake of simplicity. The Milanese believes he's been taken for a ride, and who's to say he's wrong? So he unleashes on the cabby's head a torrent of invective, opening with the words invariably employed by racists, 'I'm not a racist but ...'

Then comes the customary insults: 'We work while all you think about is thieving, you under-developed ...!' And so on and so forth. After exhausting his store of epithets, the fare finally dries up to get his breath back. Only then does the cabby put in his rejoinder: 'When you were living in caves, we were already gays.'

Though this is an urban myth, in this phrase lies all the pride that the city-dwellers derive from their conviction that, yes, all right, they have come down in the world, but only after a period of decadence before which they were masters of the planet. As a rule everyone tends to imagine that the time of his childhood was a happy time. True of individuals and of comunities. The city-dwellers have honed their sheepish pride to the point of laying claim to some unspecified aristocratic ancestry. A nostalgia that might be characterized as 'auto-exoticism': 50 per cent masturbatory, 50 per cent tending to offer an eccentric self-image. In these auto-exotic practices the city preens herself, finding herself thus original, contradictory, and picturesque, however much she has lapsed from the throne she had managed to make for herself. 'They think of themselves as gods,' wrote Tomasi di Lampedusa. And if this was not entirely true, he wasn't far off.

Precisely when this halcyon period occurred, during which the city was mistress of the world, is not easy to establish on any strictly historical basis. Some locate it between the end of the nineteenth and the beginning of the twentieth centuries, when the Tsar and the Kaiser would come to stay with the Florios, leaving their imperial vessels anchored in front of Villa Igiea. While others cultivate the memory of Frederic II, more or less claiming that it is to him that may be ascribed the last dwindling hope for a state at once lay and modern. That this sovereign's poetic sensibility went hand in hand with a certain bloodthirsty asperity is another matter, not that the city-dwellers are greatly troubled by that. What is attractive here is the man with charisma, the man who knows how to impose himself never mind the methods. If such methods are against the law, too bad: so long as he doesn't get caught out, or what kind of a man is he?

But beyond the city's blasts on her own trumpet, there was a moment when the place really did have its flash of brilliance. This was during the Arab hegemony.

The nostalgia of the city-dwellers for their own past is implicitly or explicitly of Arab making. The Arab identity is flaunted almost in your face, like the Mafia identity. That's how it is, if it seems so to us.

When you decide once and for all to leave your hotel room you will find that, at any rate, no trace of the Arab period survives in the architecture. The first thing the Norman kings did after conquering the city was to pull down the mosques and every building prior to their conquest – a meticulous blotting out of the past. This is why, in the strict meaning of the word, you'll find very little today in the way of Arabic.

Even if afterwards the Norman kings, leaving aside the arrogance of the conqueror, gave the matter thought and concluded that they had a good deal to learn from the Arabs. This is a merit that has to be recognized in the new masters of the city. Put in contact with a civilization the polar opposite of their own, they almost at once grasped that the Spartan lifestyle they had been following up till then was too wearisome by far. To fight and win wars is all very well, but what then? Whatever for? There's a saying that serves to discourage the workaholic, the man who is too little capable of taking advantage of what he gains from his labours: 'Are you trying to become the richest man in the cemetery?' So it had to be admitted: the Arabs were better at enjoying themselves.

For this reason the various Rogers and Williams took pains to avoid driving out the wisdom of the Arabs; rather they welcomed their court poets, scientists and officials, all repositories of an alien but highly attractive culture. In any case, the city was not in those days too bad a place compared with the rest of Europe. To take one example, while in the Florence of Dante the vast majority of the population was having to cope with scabies, here the unpleasant disease was far less prevalent. This was thanks to the facilities for washing and the ready availability of water, which came to the city through the hydraulic engineering of which the Arabs were masters.

Beyond appreciating their aqueducts, the Norman kings employed Arab architects first and foremost in building their so-called *pleasaunces* – little castles outside the city gates where the rulers could find distraction from the cares of government and, precisely, could take pleasure or solace themselves with their respective mistresses. Some of these houses may still be visited, though they are now totally incorporated within the built-up area. The best preserved is La Zisa – La Splendida – built for William I on a strict Arab plan.

La Cuba performed the same function; this castle was built for William II with a view to the occupation of his leisure time. Today it nests, believe it or not, amid the buildings along Corso Calatafimi, and it is a labour of imagination to evoke the park in the middle of which the castle was situated. This is where Boccaccio located his story told on 'Day Five, Sixth Tale' in the *Decameron*.

Close by we find two other small buildings of Arab inspiration from Norman times: La Cuba Soprana and Cubula, disguized within the eighteenth-century Villa Napoli.

Corso Calatafimi is the starting point for an ideal Arab-Norman tour. You have to travel its length to arrive at the cathedral of Monreale, where both Williams elected to be buried. Being a well-instructed visitor, you will have heard a good deal about the mosaics in the cathedral, and curiosity on this account should be sufficient to winkle you out of your room. Should you summon the courage to sally forth at least for a couple of hours, that is where you should head for, to the cathedral and its cloister. That is where you'll find the best example of the city's cosmopolitan nature around the year 1100: a multicultural magnetic pole where Arab, Norman and Byzantine artists worked in close collaboration and with a great capacity for stylistic synthesis. In the cloister there is a corner fountain with a stylized palm tree that is 100 per cent Arabic, for all that it is located in a Benedictine context. To describe the cathedral, only modesty prevents one from invoking other superlatives – you'll go and see for yourself.

It is generally accepted that it is thanks to this tradition of live-and-let-live, so deeply rooted in the city, that there are no records here of any major race riots. Just now and then the police take it out on illegal parkers and dark-skinned prostitutes without the citizens getting involved. Were the parkers native or the prostitutes local girls, the whole quarter would be up in arms. But for foreigners no one is going to make a fuss. Ascribe this to indifference, though, not to hostility. And that is the only symptom. For the rest, it is not a question of *tolerating* the Other, everyone simply mucks in. Nothing here in the way of social theories, no affectation of universal brotherhood. At least that has been so hitherto. In this context, too, one may read an unfortunate predisposition in the faces of the 20-year-olds. Tomorrow one of them may discover that setting a homeless man on fire or drowning a Moroccan is a trendy new way of celebrating Saturday nights. Things change, and one can place no bets on future racial harmony.

In the meantime, however, the air we breathe is so Arab-scented you'd find it hard to believe that there are no Arab monuments in the strictest sense. You've seen plenty of illustrations and the little red cupolas of many churches speak particularly clearly. But apart from the fact that they are only red thanks to capricious restoration, it is an error of historical perspective due to the fact that the Normans got the Muslims to build even their churches for them. From Norman times Arab-built churches which remain profoundly Christian include La Maggione, I Vespri, San Giovanni dei Lebbrosi, San Giovanni degli Eremiti, Santa Maria dell' Ammiraglio and San Cataldo. The little cupolas are out of keeping, merely a conceit which the new rulers did not find displeasing.

Despite the dearth of architectural relics, to get an idea of how deep was the Islamic influence on the city you have to visit The Kalsa, an area which at least on the surface offers smaller evidence of the Arab-Norman period. And yet, never more so than in this case, it is not a visit to the individual sites that counts. What counts is to stroll through the neighbourhood.

The Kalsa was originally the fortified citadel in which the emirs, in 937, established their court, on the banks of a fast-flowing stream that no longer exists, then known as Kemonia. The name of the quarter itself is Arabic: 'Al Halisa', the Elect. Even today its inhabitants speak a variant dialect crammed with *sui generis* articulations. The initial aspirate of the name, for instance, has survived. They speak of *La Hausa*. And naturally they pride themselves on their own particular quarter and its accumulated history. Even when the history that they propound is quite a story.

On 9 May 1943, Allied bombers came along to wipe out the Kalsa quarter. They arrived with bombs to destroy the old port and, while they were at it, the adjacent neighbourhood. There are photographs of the subsequent days when the Kalsa is practically non-existent. What the photos show are ruins and still more ruins. Ruins on every side. But beyond the deaths, huge destruction, and massive slaughter, the air-raid brought in its train a disaster that to this day has not been retrieved. The city discovered on that occasion that it had serious problems healing its wounds and, even before that, with staunching the blood-flow. From 1943 until today the Kalsa has continued to bleed, the degradation prevails over practically the whole quarter in spite of the various well-intentioned efforts at recovery. Hence derives the romantic impression that, in comparison with the rest of the city, the Kalsa is the part that keeps its face most pure. As though ruin were synonymous with authenticity. The modern age has brushed its margins – Via Lincoln especially – while leaving its heart intact, in the sense of spiritual and urban development. In spite of reconstruction, in the Kalsa chickens, dogs and humans still share the same living space.

Tourists wander amid buildings propped up with scaffolding. They clutch their cameras to their chests, cameras to record the insides of hovels and everything picturesque they manage to unearth, not least the poverty. Poverty is photogenic. And the Kalsa is one of those neighbourhoods euphemistically characterized as 'working class'. Or else 'a problem neighbourhood'. Cynical though it might seem, a good part of the Kalsa's allure – and of the city's, come to that – would seem to stem from its desperate state. Its best resource is disaster.

The city *is* the Kalsa; it tends to gravitate towards the neighbourhood. In the Kalsa one may trace the passage of history as one walks over it. And often it is the History that lies underfoot that can make one lose one's balance and have a bad fall. From many angles the Kalsa remains a symbol of the city as a whole. Here one may recognize the city in all its contradictions. It is a quarter with the highest concentration of Mafiosi. And yet it is here that Falcone and Borsellino were born; they played football here as children on the vast playing field provided by Piazza Magione. At the Kalsa we also find Lo Spasimo, the most recent symbol of civic pride.

The church of Santa Maria dello Spasimo never even figured in the guidebooks; most city-dwellers were unaware of its existence, or had only heard of it as a legendary, lost place. A sort of urban Atlantis. Now that the enthusiasm which greeted its reopening has died down, Lo Spasimo has become the ideal spot for wedding photos. And yet even today city-dwellers bring their guests to Lo Spasimo, and keep three paces behind them to watch them gawk at the miracle of a gigantic church open to the sky with two sumac trees that have grown up in the nave, discreetly, though, not so plumb in the centre as to inhibit theatrical or musical entertainments. Once the visitor has got over being gobsmacked, he is treated to a fabulous account of a sixteenth-century church which was never completed owing to the plague. In the course of history, Lo Spasimo has been a theatre, depot, leper clinic, and rubbish dump. The story goes that even the painting that was supposed to embellish it has quite a tale to tell. Raphael got the commission for it, to paint a Way of the Cross. But the ship conveying it hither was wrecked on its way to the island. The painting survived, miraculously, so it is said, but ended up belonging to the Spanish Crown. Today it is in the Prado.

The epic of Lo Spasimo was capped by its adventurous reopening in the mid-1990s, with tons of rubble carted away by sweated labour. It was a classic Italian-style miracle, somewhere between improvisation and programming, between voluntary action and portent. The idea was to proceed with the restoration a step at a time, for otherwise who knows when or whether the church would ever have been reopened?

Now that the major tourist streams have rediscovered it, the precincts of the convent of Lo Spasimo appear as a mixture of ruin and splendour; an example of the taste à la Piranesi for ruins restored any old how, which, in the absence of something better, would seem to characterize the city as a whole. The Teatro Garibaldi, too, on the other side of Piazza Magione, responds to this forced aesthetic criterion. Restoration proceeds as best it may, when sufficient funds are assembled. But meanwhile all over Europe people talk about the Garibaldi thanks to the shows put on by Carlo Cecchi's company – which for some years has been based here in the ruins of this crumbling theatre.

I speak to you, dear traveller, of all these things with a heart as small as could be. The truth is, there are moments when you might think you'd do better to stay right where you are. But with you it is my duty to be entirely honest. Among the things which you could not see in any event we have Lo Steri, and the fourteenth-century wooden ceiling in the Sala dei Baroni, a masterpiece out of bounds to the tourist inasmuch as the palace once belonging to the Chiaramontis is now occupied by the university administration. From Lo Steri, seat of the Inquisition, the processions set forth which often concluded in a turn about Piazza Marina followed by the incineration of the culprit.

In Piazza Marina there also occurred in March 1929 another execution, that of Joe Petrosino – an Italian-American policeman and the first of the Excellent Corpses to fall in the city's streets. On the morrow of the crime, an anonymous chisel traced a cross at the foot of the gateway to Villa Garibaldi, at the exact point where Petrosino fell. In the weeks, months, years that followed, other anonymous hands took it upon themselves to inscribe further crosses at the foot of the gateway. What anywhere else would have been merely one silly student's prank has in the city become a whole series of silly students' pranks which, all totalled up, make an authentic *damnatio memoriae*. It is hard to say how much of this is undertaken voluntarily, hard to say whether it represents any actual purpose. But the result is the same: if they had not marked the spot, no one would know exactly where Petrosino was killed, and this would represent yet another example. Heroes die and, what's more, nobody tomorrow will call them to mind.

Many are the things you would forfeit if you gave up on the Kalsa. There's the church of La Gancia, and the church of La Magione. There's the Palazzo Ajutamicristo, and there are the three churches in Via Torremuzza. There's Santa Maria della Catena. You could also take a night-time tour of the Kalsa, by car or on foot, in the noble quarters and in the most run down. Among the restaurants around Villa Garibaldi you will find that *movida* about which you will have heard so much. It would be pure and simple urbanity if the restaurants great and small did not cohabit with the improvised refreshment stalls out there to intercept tourists visiting Lo Spasimo, with the barrows deafening the streets as they hawk their pirated CDs, with prostitutes in search of clients, with those anachronistic shops that still insist on selling *scaccio*, or dried seeds and dried fruit.

Along Via Alloro, between a building site under repair and a screened-off alleyway, we pass a whole string of palazzi which just from their names give one some idea of the vanity of their past fortunes: Bonagia, Castrofilippo, Monroy della Pandolfina, Naselli d'Aragona, Faso di

San Gabriele, Rostagno di San Ferdinando. Wealth and nobility, power and prostration, day and night, life and death: every extreme touches here and survives with its opposite.

But perhaps it is this that frightens you and keeps you rooted. A fear of strong colours blended with a fear of the opposite – of being bewitched by strong colours.

10

It's do or die

This guide, of a sort, is coming to an end and here you are still barricaded in your room, wringing your hands, gazing out of the window, undecided whether to sally forth or not. If that is the case, I must be to blame, at least in part. Probably I have not succeeded in instilling in you the wish to check out for yourself whether all the damaging things said about the city are well founded. In these pages you will have met with neither confirmation nor rebuttal of these clichés, but rather a whole series of insinuations which have only served to confuse you. What one looks for in a guidebook, even a way-out one like this, are motives for taking the journey. A guidebook must love the place it is describing and must convey this passion to the reader. In this sense I must engage in a dispassionate self-criticism. One does not from these pages derive an unconditional love for the city. But not hatred either, come to that. Hopefully it does not foster a love-hate relationship, a feeling that is sometimes over-simplistic and that trumps every other feeling, when speaking about the city, especially after being there for a little while. As a rule someone who comes for a week or a month is captivated by it, and fails to understand the objections of those who are obliged to live here. This disparity of viewpoints derives from the fact that the city is like an athlete trained to run 100 metres. Over a short stretch he is able to unleash full power. But there is no point in asking a sprinter to run a marathon. The rhythm of a marathon is totally out of his reach.

Metaphors aside: the problems arise when it's a question of finding a school for one's children, a hospital if one needs medical help, a cemetery to be buried in. No point relying on the buses, but the taxis are just fine. Though to organize your daily routine on the basis of getting around by taxi is not to be thought of, for the visitor it's another matter. Therefore, coming for a short period, as in your case, you have the ideal situation in which to enjoy the best and avoid the worst, leaving that for those who are obliged to live here. Go for the best, take a taxi, forget about everything else.

Perhaps what really put you off was the description of the Kalsa. That was all it took to make you feel a sense of surfeit. The humours of this quarter can leave one stunned, if absorbed in massive doses. The Kalsa is too much. Better to cry off, and break up the visit with something more comforting. To recover your serenity, the ideal specific would be a classical monument like the Cappella Palatina, a wonder of mosaic and joinery, with a ceiling like stalactites, executed by north African craftsmen – this is one of those things that would on its own warrant the journey. If the cathedral of Monreale is lavish display on a grand scale, the little voluted chapel of Ruggero II is all for quiet recollection and small scale. It is a concentric treasure, guarded within by another treasure: Palazzo dei Normanni, today the seat of the regional parliament. Here are enacted the stratagems of island politics, on which you, foreign visitor, will have absorbed a measure of prejudice. Try to think of the Cappella Palatina.

Not far from the Palazzo dei Normanni is the cathedral, spectacular from the outside, which has been restored, but disappointing inside, which has been totally transformed. Here the Germans in particular often stop to leave a flower on the tomb of Frederick II, the sovereign who was, more than any other, the incarnation of the Teutonic character tempered by softness of the Arab influence. And incidentally, on the first column to the left of the portico, there is an inscription in Arabic to welcome the visitor. It is a *sura* from the Qur'an. There are not many churches in Christendom that can boast a passage from the Qur'an inside them.

The miniature phantasmagoria of the Cappella Palatina, the orderly calm of the Palazzo dei Normanni, the elegant contradictions of the cathedral – may these serve to reassure you? Perhaps one of the faults of this kind of guidebook is to have given scant praise to what are generally considered to be the 'monuments'. Perhaps you are one of those travellers who, the moment you arrive somewhere, likes to address the question of what there is to see. If that's the case, it is not difficult to sort out a list of the principal tourist attractions which you are going to miss if you don't get a move on.

Two of these are to be found in the museum of Palazzo Abatellis, still in the Kalsa. Antonello da Messina's *Annunciation* has been seen and reproduced many a time.

Seeing the picture itself you discover that it is but a small panel. It depicts a Madonna in a blue veil, with a lectern in front of her, and a hand slicing the air as much as to portray Mary's bewilderment at the Annunciation, but also that of the artist over his invention of a brand new perspective. Similarly brand new is the viewpoint of the watcher, the Angel-Messenger himself.

The other masterpiece in Palazzo Abatellis is *The Triumph of Death*. Let us not insist on it, but you can see that there are certain topics in this city which are taken very much to heart. The enormous fresco used to be in the atrium of Palazzo Sclafani, and is another example of the propensity for welcoming visitors by means of a memento mori. A recurring attitude. When Palazzo Sclafani was hit by a bomb, the fresco survived; it was removed from the wall, which was still standing, and after restoration was moved into the museum. It depicts Death as a skeleton mounted on horseback, the horse likewise a skeleton that gallops through the crowd. Those being transfixed by Death's arrows are the young, aristocrats, and prelates, while a happier fate is reserved for a group of the poor, who have survived to be depicted on the left of the painting. It is not known who painted this fresco. It might be Pisanello, or from his workshop, perhaps a painter from Valencia who lived in the mid-fifteenth century. His face is to be seen along with one of his assistants among the group of those saved.

The other big museum in the city is the Salinas. Here are preserved the metopes from the temples at Selinunte, which only thanks to a series of happy accidents are not today flaunting themselves in London's British Museum. The metopes were all ready to be shipped to England when, at the last moment, it was possible to block their exit. Today they feature in the city's Archaeological Museum; so if you are fond of this kind of thing, the Salinas must be one of the first calls you make.

In this list of tourist attractions, what about places that are not strictly speaking monuments? Let's say yes to this, and add the Cantieri Culturali at the Zisa, a large agglomeration of industrial archaeology acquired and restored little by little, piecemeal, one shed at a time. Were we in Paris it would have become the Centre Pompidou, plus the Grande Bibliothèque, plus a large auditorium, plus any number of theatre venues. It would have been given a grand opening ceremony *after* which it would have gone live. In the city, on the other hand, it is not clear whether any definitive plan of restoration exists, and if so in what form. Or rather: there have been several, but they have been torn up or changed time after time. They have proceeded with a partial opening, as and when there has been the will, the funds, and the time available. Some pavilions have fallen down, others are up and running, but only to a certain degree. The Cantieri provide the best symbol of the city's cultural renaissance during the 1990s, a time of great euphoria during which the town hall invested a good deal in culture. But with time the drive has weakened. The few institutions that moved in, the only ones which had any faith in the project, have quickly had a change of heart. That's because once the ferment reached its climax, satiety quickly followed. Having achieved full measure of summer reviews, festivals, Christmases and New Years, the only possibility was to go beyond this stage, regroup and press on further. In the first phase the object was to persuade the city-dwellers to leave their homes. It must be said that they came up against resistance here, similar to that which leaves you rooted to your hotel room. But they managed to overcome this. Once winkled out, once repossessed of their *joie de vivre*, it was a question of giving a sense to this mass of humanity out for an airing. *Joie de vivre* has to be nurtured. Otherwise leaving the house comes to no more than a few idlers shuffling about, and the good bureaucrat's task will be to do the opposite, not unlike the drift of so many concerned mothers: get all those people off the streets. Which is where the project of a cultural renaissance foundered. Subsequent manifestations of this kind are so ephemeral and fleeting it is quite pointless to mention them.

But there's no call to depress you even further with this kind of talk. A guidebook must not go off at tangents, it must endeavour to show off the places to visit in the most enticing light. Did we say tourist monuments? So let them be tourist monuments. Among those that best enshrine the city's pride, pride of place must go to the Teatro Massimo. Now the city-dwellers pass in front of their opera house, which they thought of as being dark grey, almost black, and are just becoming somewhat accustomed to seeing it instead in an ochre colour which was not to be thought of before 1995. They have become used to even stepping inside, and to attending the shows put on there. But to arrive at this sense of familiarity you have to negotiate a period of closure that lasted 23 years. To succeed in having it reopened required a pressure reminiscent of that in the film *Fitzcarraldo*, in which a maniac was obsessed with the idea of bringing Caruso to sing in the middle of the Amazon rain forest and eventually brought it off. When the city has the will, it is capable of this sort of epic madness.

Another miniature treasure is the Puppet Museum. Normally only those staying for a longer and deeper exploration can permit themselves a visit to what was once the private collection of Antonio Pasqualino, a singular figure, a physician fascinated with folk traditions. It is an exhibition that brings together marionettes from every corner of the globe. The core is made up of the *pupi*, which represent the local history of the theatre of figures. It might be objected that turning popular theatre into a museum piece can be depressing. But on the island, puppeteering is an almost totally uprooted tradition. True, they put on shows. But there has been no real public audience here for ages. Often it is a case of versions watered down for tourists. It would not occur to anyone nowadays to follow the sagas episode by episode that could go on for 600 episodes over a period of two years.

Today only a handful of puppeteers survive, and only one who is a true genius: Mimmo Cuticchio, who is first of all the heir to a tribe of *cuntisti*, travelling storytellers who recounted the exploits of Orlando and the French paladins. There is now only him and the Puppet Museum, and it is a long time since these two had anything approaching a cordial relationship. That often happens in the city; among people who occupy adjacent spaces, competition quickly changes to hostility. For the historical context, a museum for puppeteering is what you have to be content with.

The fact of having to make do keeps coming back. Perhaps it is this that discourages you. But in fact the opposite is the truth: this is the basic reason for which the city deserves to be known. The art of the puppeteer no longer exists, but it is worth seeing it for what it once was. A visit to the Cantieri Culturali is recommended not so much for what they are as for what they might have been and what they might yet revert to being some day. And so on. These are not values of beauty in themselves, but worthwhile for the traces of what they once were. A little like the yellow billboard at the exit from the motorway, remember?

Take the historic centre. Its fascination derives to a great extent from what is missing. From the post-war period up until today the wealthy have been abandoning it to go and settle to the north of the city. Someone has noted that from the 1950s what became decisive was the attraction of the roller blind. At a certain point the city-dwellers got fed up with shutters to their windows and decided that what they wanted were roller blinds. The dream of these blinds provoked a mass exodus from the city. The whole of the middle class went to live in the buildings along Via Sciuti and Viale Strasburgo, and so the centre became half-empty.

On this score, the city-dwellers like to remind themselves of a story: it was all the fault of the peasants, the country bumpkins who came to settle in town after the war to give the local bureaucrats something to do. They were the protagonists of this headlong rush to the worst of urbanization. They did not love the city. They had no reason to love it. As people coming in from the country, they had, in fact, every reason to hate it. Which is why they did all they could to destroy any form of beauty that had survived the bombing.

Not that this story stands up all that well, because it was the city-dwellers themselves who deserted the historic centre, nobody else. Little by little, after the houses, what collapsed were the prices of the houses remaining, and it was natural that in the four city districts the people who moved in were the down-and-outs and the incomers. The result of this is that this city, perhaps alone among cities of the globe, is one where the poor live in the middle and the well-to-do out in the suburbs.

Although change is happening, in many parts of the city centre one has the sense of crossing a ghost town. The Vucciria, for instance, has become a ghost market. Maybe the fault of over-exposure in the media which the quarter has received year in year out. There was not a film or documentary that could do without a background as picturesque as this. In time, the market traders behind their huge barrows of olives have turned into film extras. Vucciria became the fashionable place. Too many tourists, too many cameras, too many video cameras acted as a leaven on the prices. Eventually we arrived at the paradoxical situation where the locals did their shopping elsewhere. A salvage plan exists for Vucciria, just as there are for other quarters in the city. But apart from restoring buildings in danger of collapse, no plan of this kind can force shoppers to make their purchases in one quarter rather than in another.

Nowadays the more savvy tourists wander through the Vucciria market wondering whether what they are photographing is real or merely a bit of trumpery assembled for their benefit. The *banniate*, the street cries, are voices crying in the wilderness until noon, after which they pack it in. So it's better to go to the Capo, or to Ballarò, where the traders complain of lack of business, but at least they are not obliged to put on a show of work. At the Capo, the traders are traders, the shoppers are shoppers, the tomatoes are tomatoes, and the cost of a tomato is what a tomato should cost. The only surreal thing is the names of the streets: Via Sedie Volanti, Via Gioiamia, Via Scippateste. If there has to be a popular market, one may just as well shift across to the Borgo, which perhaps, owing to its position outside the historic centre, has retained its character as a perpetual commercial theatre: shopping may be indulged in at any hour of the day or night, never mind the bylaws.

Conceivably you are a rich traveller and have chosen a top hotel. This may be a reason why you are finding it hard to face the streets. If you are in the warm womb of the Hotel delle Palme, you might even let yourself be seduced by the mystique of this hotel. The staff will hasten to tell you of the time when Richard Wagner was a guest of the Hotel delle Palme, together with a retinue of family and colleagues. They will no doubt have passed in silence over the comment he made in a letter, that 'I've met only one brigand in the city – my hotelier'. Then they will have told you of other celebrities who put up here. But they'll make no mention of the great convention of Mafiosi from Europe and America which took place after the war precisely at the Hotel delle Palme.

Seeing you so reluctant to step outside, they will have told you about Baron Di Stefano, who lived in the hotel as a recluse for a good part of his life. According to the story, he had been condemned to death by the Castelvetrano 'family' on account of a murder he had unintentionally committed. On appeal, the sentence was commuted to a spell in jail. And as he was given the choice, he chose to spend the rest of his days shut away in the most luxurious hotel. In fact the story about Baron Di Stefano is no more than one of those legends that do the rounds in the city, possibly nourished by the protagonist himself, so as to turn away society invitations and justify his misanthropy. According to another version, he was also well known at Bayreuth where, being a true Wagnerian, he would never miss a performance of *Parsifal*. Only in the final phase of his life the Baron never left his room – just like you. But that was not out of choice, nor even owing to a prison term imposed by the Mafia, it was simply through illness.

Above all what they won't have told you, because it's more than the hotel's good name could afford, is of another visitor, who committed suicide in Room 224 with an overdose – the French writer Raymond Roussel. It was one 14 July, the Feast of St Rosalia, while outside the city was rocking at the height of its festive fervour.

We're not trying to hurry you, but doesn't this sound a trifle ill-omened? Is it not sufficient to make you cast aside your fears? True, there's no denying that the city is one of the few places in the West where, in the course of the 65 years of official peacetime, a war has been going on which could blaze forth again from one moment to the next, bringing about a total collapse. It would be dishonest to deny that somewhere in the city its heart of darkness is still beating.

But it is also true that the rest of the world cultivates a conception of the city that is quite scary, and by and large mythical. In the first edition of the *Encyclopedia*, under the appropriate heading, we would read: 'Ancient city destroyed by an earthquake.' An error, a misprint. But ever since, its inhabitants have had to demonstrate that they are still alive and in good health.

If you're looking for a spur to action, look for it right here, in the possibility that while you are tormenting yourself in the fastness of your hotel room, what is happening outside is one of those portentous events that the city always keeps up its sleeve. Supposing it was an earthquake, do you think you'd get away with sheltering under a roof? Giovanni Falcone was once asked whether he was afraid of being killed. He answered that fear was a human emotion, but one must not let oneself be conditioned by it. What he actually said, quoting Shakespeare, was, 'Cowards die many times before their death/The valiant never taste of death but once.' Let us state it frankly: the fascination of the city lies precisely in the fact that to survive is now possible, but not yet a matter of course.

You will have heard plenty of stories about the city. This guide, too, will have contributed a few which, if not completely untrue, are not far off. But assuredly they are related here as the very truth, and it is not long before this kind of story becomes true by virtue of sheer repetition.

Once upon a time a writer called Paco Ignacio Taibo II said that, he knew not why, but the island seemed to him an onion. It is made up of layers. Each time you peel off a layer there is another one beneath it, time after time. How right he was! That is how the island is. And the city is, too. You can take it as you find it, with its outer skin. It is a beautiful thing, with its own eccentric perfection. It's an onion, no doubt about it. You may settle for the definition you have been given of it, and rest content with that. But you can also try to peel off the outer layer, and you'll still have an onion, but with the colour and shape slightly altered. You can slice off the top and bottom, to help you with the operation you are trying out. Here you might have a problem, because the onion starts to make you weep. Your tears go beyond emotion, they are a conditioned reflex. Never mind! This too is commonplace: peel an onion and you'll start to weep.

The very outer layer does need peeling off, because it's always a bit too tough to be digested. Keep going. Beneath it is another layer that seems a bit better, of a lighter colour. Your fry-up, if that's what it is, can be made with it. However, if the onion is needed for a salad, better peel off this layer too. In any case, curiosity tends to prevail and on you go, layer after layer. You keep peeling the onion and are surprised each time by the new nuance of rosy white you uncover. None of the layers you peel off alters the substance of the onion. It started out an onion, and an onion it remains, even if now it is a rarefied onion, much more refined. Peel off another layer, and another. In the light of each layer you remove, the previous one looks coarse. Had you remained satisfied with that one, how wrong you would have been, because the one beneath it seems to you still more authentic, in its rarefaction. Until, at a certain point, you feel you have come upon the perfect essence of the onion. The bulb of the bulb. The distillation of the distillation of the distillation of the onion. But there is still the very finest skin which you can remove, and your perfectionism carries you on to discover what lies beneath that one. You peel it off with extreme care and discover that what lies underneath is nothing. One layer before and it was still an onion, the most perfect onion, and one layer after and there's nothing left. You can't use it for a fry-up nor for a salad. There's nothing you can do with it.

In the same way you have to consider what you know about the city. You can decide to stop at a certain layer and be satisfied with that. The fry-up or the salad will still be fine. But if you are the good traveller I take you to be, you have to press on and try peeling off a few more layers. And *you* must be the one to do it. Even if peeling the onion makes you weep, you cannot leave the task to others in your place. They don't know at which layer of the onion you want to stop, they don't know to what use you mean to put the onion, and they risk peeling off layer after layer and throwing them out even if they are good.

Above all they risk peeling away that final ultra-delicate layer beyond which the onion ceases to be an onion. The city is no longer the city.

I'm happy to see you stopping to think. Take all the time you need before deciding which layer of the onion is the one you need for your purposes. But then stand up. Take your overcoat if you feel the need for it. Leave your room. Go downstairs. Say hello to the hall porter, grasp the door handle and press it downwards. Open the door.

At once the light surrounds you.

You're right, I've filled your head with idle chatter, but I've forgotten to set you on your guard against the light of the city. A savage light which, at certain times of day, can stab the eyes of those unaccustomed to it. But don't succumb now to a fresh panic. You can always buy sunglasses.

And then it is right that you should know that there are so many things not mentioned in these pages. I've neglected, for instance, to stress the sheer beauty of certain places. On certain details of banal splendour there seemed to me no point in dwelling. On the other hand you can be sure that I've hidden nothing that could alarm you. Therefore, don't be alarmed. Now you're out in the street, the big step is taken. As for the things I've forgotten to tell you, too bad! It simply means you'll find them out for yourself.